BRIGHTER DAYS AHEAD

Looking Beyond Today's Troubles

Published By
Help4U Publications
Chesterton, IN

HELP4U
PUBLICATIONS

Brighter Days Ahead: Looking Beyond Today's Troubles
by David J. Olson
Copyright©2019 by David J. Olson

ISBN 978-1-940089-31-7

Library of Congress Control Number: 2019919708

www.help4Upublications.com

<u>Credits</u>: Cover Photo from Lightstock

All rights reserved. No part of this publication may be reproduced or transmitted in any form, except for brief quotation in review, without written permission from the publisher.

All Scripture quotations are from the *King James Bible*.

<u>Disclaimer</u>: The content of this book is for educational and informational purposes only. Opinions and suggestions are not intended to be nor should they be considered as medical, psychiatric, or legal advice. Neither the author nor the publisher are medical professionals and are not responsible for the medical or mental health decisions made by the reader.

DEDICATION

To my Dad, Roger Olson –
Thank you for teaching me to look to the Lord during trying times. You often said, *"In every thing give thanks…"* (1 Thessalonians 5:18). You have lived what you preached, and your testimony has been an example and encouragement to many.

In memory of my Mom, Judy Olson –
Mom was full of love and concern for others. She made great sacrifices for her family and prayed faithfully for all of us. Losing her was difficult, but with the Lord, there are always *Brighter Days Ahead!*

Contents

Introduction	7
1: When Darkness Comes	11
2: It's Not God's Fault	15
3: Asking Why	21
4: Reasons Why	25
5: God Is for Me	31
6: Facing Life's Disappointments	35
7: There's Hope	39
8: Blessed Mourning	43
9: Anxious Thoughts	47
10: Rejoicing in Trials	53
11: The Way Up Is Down	57
12: The Day of Trouble	61
13: God's Exchange Program	67
14: Beauty for Ashes	71
15: The Oil of Joy	77
16: The Garment of Praise	83
17: Never Alone	89
18: Wait on the Lord	93
19: Light My Candle	99
20: Good from Grief	103
21: Battling Bitterness	107
22: Waves of Affliction	115
23: Promised Rest	121
24: Painful Loss	125

25: The Spirit of Fear 129
26: The Furnace of Affliction 135
27: Give Thanks 141
28: The Path to Discouragement 145
29: Feeling Guilty 153
30: Why Are You Troubled? 159
31: Renewed 163
Appendix A: Help Begins with Salvation 173
Appendix B: Helpful Verses 177

Introduction

Nobody is exempt from heartaches and hardships. Throughout the history of the world, people have battled grief, discouragement, fear, and anxiety. When handled correctly, trials can draw us closer to the Lord and build our faith. Unfortunately, instead of turning to God, many people turn against Him.

Because God loves us, He has a plan for each of our troubles. His wisdom and concern are clearly revealed in Scripture—*"But though he cause grief, yet will he have compassion according to the multitude of his mercies. For he doth not afflict willingly nor grieve the children of men"* (Lamentations 3:32-33). He gains no pleasure from afflicting His children. He only allows suffering when He knows it is best. It is our duty to trust Him. Although storm clouds may overshadow us at times, God promises that there are brighter days ahead. By faith, we must rest upon His Word.

The purpose of this book is not merely to put a positive spin on problems. My goal is to challenge people to see their trials as God sees them and react as He has instructed. The Bible is a Book about real people with real problems and offers real solutions. Rather than trust the ever-changing philosophies of man, we must depend upon the never-changing principles of God. The truths of Scripture are tried and proven. They have helped people for thousands of years and cannot be improved upon.

Although others may have failed you, God will never do so! *"It is better to trust in the Lord than to put confidence in man"* (Psalm 118:8).

Some people think that only weak-minded and emotionally unstable people are affected by fear, anxiety, grief, and discouragement. Such thinking is nonsense. Great heroes of the faith battled their emotions. Joshua had to be reminded repeatedly not to fear. Job experienced great loss and deep sorrow. David was no stranger to fear, grief, and discouragement. Paul admitted that he had fears within his heart. Timothy appeared to have a timid disposition. These mighty men of God learned to trust the Lord for help in times of weakness, and we can too. There is hope!

Unfortunately, the stigma associated with emotional problems prevents many people from seeking help. Instead of dealing with their troubles Biblically, far too many people spiral deeper and deeper into hopelessness. When this happens, every area of life is affected. Sorrow can have negative effects on our physical, mental, and spiritual health. In extreme cases, some people lose their desire to live and contemplate suicide. Obviously, God does not want us to plunge to such depths of despair. Admitting that you are weak is a sign of strength, not an indication of weakness. Failing to acknowledge and address your frailties is the worst kind of weakness. If you deal with them properly, they can become a source of blessing. Paul learned that God's *"strength is made perfect in weakness"* (2 Corinthians 12:9).

Finding peace in life's storms is often a journey. When patterns of negative thinking and wrong reactions to trials become entrenched in our lives, it takes time to overcome them. Proper thinking patterns must be established. Renewing your mind daily through God's Word is vital. Because this book is packed with Scripture, it can help you think clearly when you face trials. *Brighter Days Ahead* contains thirty-one encouraging chapters. By reading one chapter each day, you can begin to develop a positive attitude over a month's time. Whether you read this book as part of your daily devotions or straight through in a few evenings, you will discover that the Lord will never fail you.

The truths contained in this book have seen me through many dark days, and I am confident they will help you too. Allow the promises and principles of Scripture to comfort and challenge you. God's ways work! May the Lord bless you as you look for brighter days ahead!

"For thou wilt light my candle:
the LORD my God will enlighten my
darkness" -Psalm 18:28.

Day One

When Darkness Comes

"For the enemy hath persecuted my soul; he hath smitten my life down to the ground; he hath made me to dwell in darkness, as those that have been long dead"
—Psalm 143:3.

David's enemy plotted to kill him. The persecution was so severe that David already felt like his foe had been successful, saying, *"...he hath smitten my life down to the ground."* Obviously, David was still alive, but he felt as good as dead. Have you ever felt that way? Like David, we have an enemy who wants to destroy us—*"the devil, as a roaring lion, walketh about, seeking whom he may devour"* (1 Peter 5:8). Satan's attacks can be so fierce and relentless that we sometimes feel defeated as David did.

How Darkness Affects Us

This psalm shows the real battle that God's people have with discouragement at times. In David's heart, the sun was obscured by clouds. His trouble was so bad that it seemed like he had been made *"to dwell in darkness."* Our trials may be different than David's, but the devil's tactics are the same. He attempts to paint the picture as gloomy as possible, knowing that darkness brings fear, torment, and panic. When we begin to see life as Satan has shaded it, we lose our joy. The devil knows that *"the joy of the LORD is your strength"* (Nehemiah 8:10). If we allow discouragement to set in, we become weak and ineffective in God's service. As David found himself in such a condition, we will too one day. Let's see how he handled it.

What to Do When In Darkness

Thankfully, when David saw his condition was bleak, he did not quit. He was weak, but not defeated. Paul mentioned that we are sometimes *"cast down, but not destroyed"* (2 Corinthians 4:9). Notice four actions that David took that can help us too.

First, he remembered—*"I remember the days of old"* (Psalm 143:5). He thought about what God had already done for him. Things had not always been dark. Like David, you have enjoyed God's blessings in the past. Rehearsing the Lord's mercies takes your mind off your miseries. Considering the goodness shown in prior days will renew your hope that brighter days are on the horizon. What God did in the past, He is able to do again! Take time to *"remember the days of old"* and be thankful for them.

Second, he meditated—*"I meditate on all thy works"* (Psalm 143:5). David expanded his thinking to include all of God's works, not just what the Lord had done for him. This also shows faith. As we see what God has done for others, we gain confidence that He can do likewise for us. Has the Lord lifted other saints out of darkness? Certainly! This gives us hope that He will display His power for us in the same way. After all, *"God is no respecter of persons"* (Acts 10:34).

Third, he mused—*"I muse on the work of thy hands"* (Psalm 143:5). The word *muse* refers to thinking so deeply that you become unaware of what is going on around you. David's thoughts about the Lord progressively got stronger. As he remembered what God had done and meditated on what the Lord could do, he found himself in the presence of God. He became so focused on the Lord that he lost sight of his darkness. All he began to see was light proceeding from God. Oh, that we would think so much about the Lord that we forget our troubles and see His goodness! What a cure! Nothing renews our minds and focuses our attention on the Lord like meditating on His Word. When we do that, our darkness turns to day. David was not the only one who displayed this attitude. The apostle Paul was able to rejoice while in prison. By faith, we can find hope and peace when the storm clouds of life overshadow us.

> When we focus on the Lord's blessings, we tend to forget about our burdens.

Fourth, he prayed—*"I stretch forth my hands unto thee"* (Psalm 143:6). Because David's heart was so focused on the Lord, he lifted his hands in dependence and expectancy. This provides a beautiful picture of hope. As a little child, you can stretch your hand up to your heavenly Father. He will grasp it and lead you through your dark valley. Open your other hand and stretch it out to receive a blessing from God's giving hand. Prayer provides guidance and provision for our times of trouble.

Looking Past the Darkness

David anticipated help from above and ended the psalm with words of faith. He said, *"I am thy servant"* (Psalm 143:12). Though Satan sought to sideline him through dark days, David focused on the Lord. What were the results? His strength was renewed, and his service was restored. God wants to revitalize your life too. Don't give up. He still has work for you to do. Reaffirm your dedication to the Lord by saying, *"I am thy servant."* Then, get busy doing His will once again.

Conclusion

Though Satan would have us *"to dwell in darkness,"* there are steps that we can take to be delivered from discouragement. Your strength may be small right now, but as you begin to think on God's blessings, you will think less on your burdens. Remember the happy times you once enjoyed, and realize that God has many more of them in store for you. Once your focus is adjusted towards heaven, you will find your heart striking a different tune. There are brighter days ahead!

Day Two

It's Not God's Fault

"He is the Rock, his work is perfect: for all his ways are judgment: a God of truth and without iniquity, just and right is he" —Deuteronomy 32:4.

Life is filled with troubles, disappointments, and injustices. Words fail to describe the feelings of those who suffer overwhelming losses. A sense of hopelessness often sets in. Life loses purpose. Light has been shut out and darkness prevails within. The bitter pain causes important relationships to suffer. The strife in heart and home seems almost too much to bear. Does that describe you? Oh, for a solution to the present trouble and relief from continual heartache!

For some, heartbreaking tragedies strike when least expected, leaving pain and confusion. Lives are lost or greatly altered through disease, natural disasters, war, and accidents. It is even worse when intentional harm is inflicted. The thought that runs through the minds of many people is, "Why did God let this happen?" It is amazing how quickly the Lord gets blamed for all the trouble in the world. Why not blame the devil or evil people in the world? It makes more sense to realize that bad things come from bad sources. Let us consider our reactions to trouble.

Some psychologists suggest that there are five stages of grief: denial, anger, bargaining, depression, and acceptance. While theories differ on how people grieve, what is important is that people accept their loss and begin to live a fruitful life again. Having ministered to individuals during their times of grief, I have learned that people grieve differently. There are not five definite stages that people have to pass through in order to find peace. It would be cruel to think God expects us to have problems with anger and depression in order to be well. Negative emotions make our problems worse, not better. As we will see, God's way is much better. Unfortunately, not everyone seeks the Lord as they should. Some battle depression and hopelessness, while others seem to be angry at the world. Many people carry a heavy load of guilt, thinking they should have done something to prevent their loss. The combination of symptoms varies greatly. Sadly, the world is filled with people who have never come to a place of acceptance, often harboring bitterness towards God.

> Anger towards God usually leads to anger issues with others.

When someone becomes angry at God, they usually develop anger issues in other relationships. For example, consider a middle-aged man who loses his wife and blames God. Before his loss, he was even-tempered, but after the passing of his wife, he loses his temper with his children quicker than he used to. The problem is not with God, nor is it necessarily with his children. The problem is with him.

He allowed his grief to lead to anger. Oh, if we could all realize how harmful it is to be upset with the Lord!

Perhaps you have suffered a devastating loss, and the pain in your heart seems unbearable. You don't know if you can ever be happy again. Please understand that you will never find true peace by blaming God. The passage at the beginning of our reading reminds us that the Lord is incapable of doing anything wrong—*"He is the Rock, his work is perfect: for all his ways are judgment: a God of truth and without iniquity, just and right is he."* He is without sin. He is fair. He is always right. Further, *"God is love"* (1 John 4:8). He is not the source of your darkness—*"God is light, and in him is no darkness at all"* (1 John 1:5). He gives joy and gladness—*"...the God of hope fill you with all joy and peace in believing, that ye may abound in hope"* (Romans 15:13). The Lord helps those who hurt within—*"He healeth the broken in heart, and bindeth up their wounds"* (Psalm 147:3).

God did not make evil. He created a perfect world—*"And God saw every thing that he had made, and, behold, it was very good"* (Genesis 1:31). There was no sin, sickness, or sadness. Everything was *"very good."* What ruined things? Mankind disobeyed God. Since then, all of our troubles have resulted from sin. At times we reap the consequences of our own sinful actions, and other times we suffer because of the sin of others. It is not God's fault. Thankfully, He has made a way for us to find forgiveness through His Son, Jesus. By repenting of our sin and receiving Jesus as our Savior, we will get to experience perfect happiness in heaven. Jesus left heaven, lived a perfect life, willingly suffered punishment for our sins, and rose again. He promised, *"In my Father's house are many mansions: if it were not so, I would have told you. I go to prepare a place for you. And if I go and prepare a place for you, I will come again, and receive you unto myself; that where I am, there ye may be also"* (John 14:2-3). God loves us so much that He made a way that we can enter heaven where there will be no more suffering. However, if we refuse to make peace with Him, eternal torment awaits us.

If you have not received Jesus as your Savior, please do so today. A new life of joy and hope awaits! Take Him at His promise, *"Come unto me, all ye that labour and are heavy laden, and I will give you rest...and ye shall find rest unto your souls"* (Matthew 11:28-29). Isn't that what you want? (See Appendix A to learn more about salvation.)

Perhaps you are already a Christian but have allowed bitterness into your heart. The Lord is ready to cleanse and restore you. Like David, you can pray, *"Make me to hear joy and gladness...Restore unto me the joy of thy salvation"* (Psalm 51:8, 12).

God's Word abounds with principles and promises that have brought comfort and rest to countless believers. We do not have to needlessly live with guilt, anger, and depression. Allow *"the God of all comfort"* to bring healing to your heart (2 Corinthians 1:3). Let us never fall into Satan's trap of finding fault with God. The devil whispers in our ears, "It's God's fault," because he seeks to prevent us from finding relief through God. Satan wants us miserable. Have you seen that your misery has come from the devil, not God? If you have questioned God's goodness, are you ready to swallow your pride and admit you have been wrong? If so,

> *"...the God of all comfort"* longs to heal your hurting heart.

He promises, *"And ye shall seek me, and find me, when ye shall search for me with all your heart"* (Jeremiah 29:13). Seek Him without delay, and soon you will be able to say, *"Truly God is good"* (Psalm 73:1)!

"He shall call upon me, and I will answer him: I will be with him in trouble; I will deliver him, and honour him"
-Psalm 91:15.

Day Three

Asking Why

"For thou art the God of my strength: why dost thou cast me off? why go I mourning because of the oppression of the enemy?" —Psalm 43:2.

When troubles overwhelm us, the first question that often comes to mind is why. We ask, "Why did this have to happen? Why me? Why now?" Some people warn us never to question God or ask why. In the Bible, we see bad men and good men asking why. In some cases, God punished people for asking why, and in other instances, He answered their questions. This shows us that asking why can be unacceptable sometimes and acceptable at other times. So, when is it okay to ask God why? Well, it is actually not a matter of *when* but *how* we ask.

Nowhere in Scripture do we see that we are forbidden to ask God why. In fact, our Savior asked a *why* question of His Father. When suffering on the cross He cried, *"My God, my God, why hast thou forsaken me?"* (Matthew 27:46). Obviously, Jesus already knew why. He was dying for the sin of the world, but knowing that did not make it any easier. His *why* was an expression of grief. It was not a request for information, nor was it a cry of dissatisfaction with His Father's will. In His affliction, He identified with humanity and showed that it is natural to ask why when grieving. Like our Lord, we will also be overwhelmed with burdens at times and be moved to express our heartaches through prayer. When we do, we must ensure that we maintain the right attitude.

Asking why can either show faith in God or express fault with God. How we ask determines how God responds. When we speak to the Lord in humility, He welcomes our questions. However, when our hearts are haughty, He corrects us. Let's consider two basic attitudes people have when asking God why.

Asking Why Can Show Dependence Upon God

The Psalms record many instances in which people cried out to God in anguish. Though they asked why, they did so with humble hearts. For instance, Psalm 10 begins with two *why* questions, *"Why standest thou afar off, O LORD? why hidest thou thyself in times of trouble?"* (10:1). Taken at face value, we might think the psalmist was upset with God. However, nothing could be further from the truth. He was crying out in desperation for the Lord's help. Notice his faith in God—*"The LORD is King for ever and ever"* (10:16). Consider also his confidence that God would help—*"LORD, thou hast heard the desire of the humble…thou wilt cause thine ear to hear"* (10:17). He asked why because he did not understand what God was doing, but he maintained faith that He was still in control.

Moses also asked why when things were not going well. The children of Israel were slaves in Egypt, and God commanded Moses to confront Pharaoh and demand Israel's freedom. Instead of letting them go, Pharaoh oppressed the people even more. To make matters worse, the children of Israel saw Moses as the source of their troubles, not the solution to them. Moses had obeyed the Lord, and things only seemed to get worse! With a heavy heart, he prayed, *"Why is it that thou hast sent me?"* (Exodus 5:22). He sought clarification. Because he cried out to God looking for direction, the Lord heard him. With reassurance, God responded, *"Now shalt thou see what I will do to Pharaoh"* (Exodus 6:1). Like Moses, we will suffer heartaches and disappointments when following the Lord. However, if we humbly seek His assistance, He will strengthen us as He did Moses.

| If we humbly ask why, God will not reject our cries.

Asking Why Can Express Dissatisfaction With God

Some people are prone to find fault with God's plan for their lives. They get upset with the Lord when things don't go the way they think they should. Instead of turning to God for help, they turn against Him. Their *why* questions are cries of rebellion, not pleas for mercy. Consider an example. The Lord had delivered the children of Israel from bondage in Egypt. While in route to the Promised Land, God miraculously provided food and water for them. Instead of being grateful, they complained about His provision. They despised the Lord, the manna He had given, and the deliverance He had provided. In their hearts, they wanted to return to Egypt. They cried, *"Why came we forth out of Egypt?"* (Numbers 11:20). They were defiant and opposed to God's will for their lives. What followed? *"The wrath of God came upon them"* (Psalm 78:31). If you resist the Lord, He will resist you.

Consider another warning in Scripture about asking why. *"O man, who art thou that repliest against God? Shall the thing formed say to him that formed it, Why hast thou made me thus?"* (Romans 9:20). Are you ever tempted to complain about how the Lord made you? Perhaps you think you were shortchanged in some way, wishing you had better looks, intellect, health, talent, opportunities, etc. Be very careful not to question God's wisdom.

> Don't find fault with God's plan for your life.

When we say, "Lord, why did you make me this way?" we are finding fault with Him. In fact, we are speaking *"against God."* If you have asked why inappropriately, you are in direct opposition to the Lord and cannot expect deliverance from your troubles. Humble yourself and seek His help. *"God resisteth the proud, but giveth grace unto the humble"* (James 4:6).

Conclusion

When troubles enter our lives, it is natural to ask why. Jesus did it, and He expects us to do the same. However, our *whys* must be a sign of dependence on God, not a sign of disgust with Him. Our prayers must express faith in the Lord, not find fault with Him. Instead of being upset with God because of your circumstances, learn to trust Him. Faith not only changes your outlook on life, but it secures God's blessing in your time of trouble. Those who trust Him will find that *"he is a rewarder of them that diligently seek him"* (Hebrews 11:6). Faith makes all the difference!

Day Four

Reasons Why

"Knowing this, that the trying of your faith worketh patience. But let patience have her perfect work, that ye may be perfect and entire, wanting nothing" —James 1:3-4.

Now that we have considered our attitude when asking why, let's turn our attention to God's answers. Though tragedies often make no sense to us, they never take the Lord by surprise. God has a reason for every trial that He allows us to endure. We may not know why immediately, but in due time God's purpose is usually apparent. For example, the church in Jerusalem grieved over the stoning of Stephen. However, that persecution was used to spread the gospel in a mighty way (Acts 8:1-8). Further, Stephen's testimony appears to have been an instrumental factor in the conversion of Saul of Tarsus, who became the author of much of the New Testament. God used an unbelievably tragic event to further His kingdom in ways never imagined.

It would be nice if every trial came with a note from heaven, describing the exact reason for it. Unfortunately, it does not work that way. However, the Bible reveals some typical ways that God uses trials in our lives. Perhaps one of the following reasons fits your situation.

Trials Are Used to Build Our Faith

Paul understood that trials make us stronger. He said, *"...we glory in tribulations also: knowing that tribulation worketh patience; and patience, experience; and experience, hope* (Romans 5:3-4). Troubles produce helpful virtues like patience, experience, and hope. It could be that God is using your affliction to teach you to trust Him in a greater way. The more you see His deliverance, the stronger your faith becomes.

Trials Are Used to Refine Us

The Lord likes to make useful servants more fruitful. Jesus said, *"...every branch that beareth fruit, he purgeth it, that it may bring forth more fruit"* (John 15:2). Christians are like trees in an orchard. They must be pruned in order to yield more fruit. As a farmer cuts off superfluous branches with a sharp instrument, God uses trials to refine us. A perfect example of this is Job. Though he was a man with an impeccable testimony (Job 1:1), the Lord chose to make him even better through a series of troubling events. Despite suffering great loss and battling discouragement, Job understood God's purpose for his trial.

> God's refining fire purifies.

He declared, *"But he knoweth the way that I take: when he hath tried me, I shall come forth as gold"* (Job 23:10). Job knew that he would be better because of his troubles. Oh, that we would echo the words of Job when we find ourselves in the refiner's fire! Why does God allow trials? He wants us to *"come forth as gold"*—bright and valuable for His service.

Trials Are Used to Prepare Us to Help Others

Paul understood that the experience gained through trials can greatly benefit other believers. He said, *"...the God of all comfort...comforteth us in all our tribulation, that we may be able to comfort them which are in any trouble, by the comfort wherewith we ourselves are comforted of God"* (2 Corinthians 1:3-4). Here's how it works. God allows tribulation, He provides comfort, and this equips us to help others who face the same problem. Stop and think how your trouble can be a blessing to people in need. In reality, our trials can prepare us to bring relief to countless numbers of individuals in the future. That makes *"the trial of your faith...precious"* (1 Peter 1:7). Learn to highly treasure your trials and see them as opportunities to help others.

Trials Are Used to Reach Others With the Gospel

When Paul and Silas were beaten and imprisoned for preaching the gospel, it hardly seemed fair. However, instead of complaining, they *"sang praises unto God"* (Acts 16:25). Not long afterwards, they discovered that the Lord had a divine appointment for them. The keeper of the prison had lost all hope and was about to take his own life. After the men of God intervened, the jailor cried out, *"Sirs, what must I do to be saved?"* (Acts 16:30). That night, he trusted Christ as Savior along with *"all his house"* (Acts 16:34). God used the troubles of Paul and Silas to bring several souls to Himself. The Lord may allow your troubles to bring you in contact with lost souls too. When He does, look for opportunities to tell them about Jesus. Your temporary troubles may lead to eternal salvation for others.

Trials Are Used to Shame the Devil

An unseen battle is waged behind the scenes of everyday life. Spiritual conflict invisible to mortal eyes plays a part in our trials. Satan opposes God and does his best to slander the Lord's servants. He is known as *"the accuser of our brethren"* (Revelation 12:10). The account of Job illustrates this unseen warfare. After the Lord described Job as *"a perfect and an upright man, one that feareth God, and escheweth evil"* (Job 1:8), the devil began his smear campaign. He proposed that Job only feared God because of the blessings he received. Then he challenged God, *"But put forth thine hand now, and touch all that he hath, and he will curse thee to thy face"* (Job 1:11). As we know, the Lord allowed Satan to afflict His beloved servant to prove the devil wrong. After Job lost his children, his wealth, and his health, he remained faithful to God. We read, *"In all this Job sinned not, nor charged God foolishly"* (Job 1:22). The Lord used Job to deal a blow to the devil, and He rewarded Job handsomely for his faithfulness—*"...the LORD gave Job twice as much as he had before"* (Job 42:10). As Job did not see the spiritual battle going on behind the scenes, we may not either. However, we can be assured that remaining faithful to God during our trials can be a source of grief to the devil. If you think such a scenario is unlikely in the life of a Christian, think again. Did not the Lord promise, *"And the God of peace shall bruise Satan under your feet shortly"* (Romans 16:20)? When our trials advance Christ's kingdom, we ought to rejoice to be counted worthy of such an honor.

> God can use His children to deal a blow to the devil.

Trials Are Used for the Glory of God

When Jesus travelled with His disciples one day, they came upon a man which had been blind since birth. The disciples immediately thought the worst and asked, *"Master, who did sin, this man, or his parents, that he was born blind?"* (John 9:2). Jesus responded, *"Neither hath this man sinned, nor his parents: but that the works of God should be made manifest in him"* (John 9:3). The reason the man was blind was not because he or his parents had sinned but so that God could perform a miracle. God used the man's suffering to bring glory to Himself. The Lord may have similar plans for your troubles. When you begin to wonder why He allows you to endure great hardships, it may be because He plans to show Himself mighty on your behalf. In the end, He is exalted and we are blessed. What a wise God we have! Be patient and wait for the Lord to work.

Conclusion

As we have seen, the Scriptures reveal that there are many possible reasons the Lord allows us to experience trials. Instead of being selfish and complaining about our troubles, we should submit to the One who knows what is best for us. Whatever the reason for your present problem, the Lord has a plan for it. In the end, you will discover that it is a good one.

"The LORD is on my side; I will not fear: what can man do unto me?" -Psalm 118:6.

Day Five

God Is for Me

"When I cry unto thee, then shall mine enemies turn back: this I know; for God is for me" —Psalm 56:9.

Have you ever felt like everything or everyone was against you? What a dreadful feeling that is! Before David became king, he knew what it was like to have enemies. King Saul and the armies of Israel relentlessly hunted him throughout the nation. David's trouble was not imagined. He was forced to live in exile, travel through the wilderness, and hide in caves. Despite the very real dangers he faced, his faith was strong. He continued to seek the Lord and was assured of deliverance. He expressed his faith, saying, *"When I cry unto thee, then shall mine enemies turn back: this I know; for God is for me."* Despite his troubles, he knew that God was still on his side.

While it is unlikely that you have an entire army against you, your foes are still real. Whether they are people at work, in your home, around the neighborhood, or within your church, the rejection you experience is troubling. Perhaps your distress is caused by circumstances, not individuals. One trial after another seems to pile upon you. If anything can go wrong, it goes wrong. You have rewritten Murphy's Law, replacing your name for Murphy's. If that describes you, you are not alone.

In the Bible, a man named Jacob felt like all was against him. After experiencing a famine in the land, he sent his sons to Egypt to find food for their families. When one of the rulers in Egypt demanded that Benjamin, Jacob's youngest son, be brought to Egypt, Jacob could take no more. He exclaimed, *"Me have ye bereaved of my children: Joseph is not, and Simeon is not, and ye will take Benjamin away: all these things are against me"* (Genesis 42:36). Though he had notable trials, he was wrong to think all was against him. He had lost sight of God in his troubles and failed to believe that the Lord had a plan for his hardships. As we know, the ruler who requested Benjamin's presence was actually Jacob's son Joseph. In reality, Jacob lost none of his children, and God used his troubles to miraculously provide for his family.

> God has a plan for your trials. He is for you!

What a contrast we see between Jacob and David. When Jacob was overwhelmed, he said, *"…all these things are against me."* David, on the other hand, responded, *"…this I know…God is for me."* Both encountered unbelievably difficult circumstances, but their outlooks were quite different. Jacob experienced fear and frustration. David had confidence and comfort. Which describes you when you are overwhelmed with problems? Unfortunately, many believers respond like Jacob rather than as David did.

When it seems like all are against you, think again. Like David, we should learn to say, *"God is for me."* It may not seem like it at the moment, but we are encouraged to walk by faith, not by sight. What we see naturally is trouble, but the eye of faith sees a loving heavenly Father Who watches over us. Even when strong foes oppose us, we can be victorious. The next time all seems against you, remember the words of the apostle Paul—*"If God be for us, who can be against us?"* (Romans 8:31). Notice that Paul posed a question. The obvious answer is that, with God by our side, nobody can be against us!

The psalmist cried out, *"The LORD is on my side; I will not fear: what can man do unto me?"* (Psalm 118:6). With renewed faith, let us not fear our oppressors or the outcome of our battles. Let us be convinced of God's assistance and declare, *"The LORD is on my side."*

You are going to have a bad day from time to time. In fact, you may have several bad days in a row. Not everyone will appreciate you. Sometimes your service for God will not be welcomed. At times, it will seem like unfavorable circumstances and opposition will be your payment for good deeds. How will you respond? Will you complain, or will you see that God has a plan for your trouble? Will you say, *"all these things are against me"* or *"God is for me"*? If your faith has faltered, confess it at once and renew your confidence in the Mighty God!

"From the end of the earth will I cry unto thee, when my heart is overwhelmed: lead me to the rock that is higher than I." -Psalm 61:2.

Day Six

Facing Life's Disappointments

> "And David was greatly distressed; for the people spake of stoning him, because the soul of all the people was grieved, every man for his sons and for his daughters: but David encouraged himself in the LORD his God"
> —1 Samuel 30:6.

Despite what proponents of the prosperity gospel say, God does not promise a problem-free life. Even the most faithful servants of the Lord will be greatly distressed at times. David is a great example of this. Although he was a man after God's own heart, he was not exempt from great hardships. If great men of God have suffered, so will we. However, when we handle life's disappointments properly, we will secure God's blessing from every trial we encounter. It is never the Lord's intention to harm us but to help us.

While David and his men dwelt in the land of the Philistines to escape from King Saul, God preserved them from having to enter battle against the Israelites. It was a tremendous relief not to be forced to fight against their own countrymen. However, when they returned to their camp in Ziklag, they discovered that the Amalekites had burned the city with fire and taken the women and children captive.

Great Distress

David faced a great difficulty. We read that he was greatly distressed. To be distressed means to suffer tremendous pain. David and his men had lost their wives and children. Can you imagine the heartache they suffered? Consider their response: *"Then David and the people that were with him lifted up their voice and wept, until they had no more power to weep"* (I Samuel 30:4).

When not handled Biblically, pain and sorrow often lead to irrational behavior. David's men were not necessarily all spiritual men, and their reaction to the crisis put David in great danger—*"the people spake of stoning him."* It was absurd for the men to blame David for their loss. After all, he was their leader, not their enemy. Always be careful not to lash out at those who are on your side. The men needed David's help, but they took their grief out on him. Resist the temptation to make rash decisions or turn against those who can help you during your times of affliction. Check your life right now. Have you developed wrong attitudes or behavior because of failing to handle your problems Scripturally?

> When things look down, look up!

Great Decision

Thankfully, David did not react the same way that his men had done. Instead, he made a great decision—*David encouraged himself in the LORD his God.* Rather than feeling sorry for himself, David did the right thing by going straight to the Lord. Notice that he did not encourage himself by looking within his own heart for strength, nor did he look outwardly at the circumstances. David did what we should do—look up! Too often when trials come into our lives, we are tempted to focus on our situation; but encouragement will only come as we turn to the Lord.

Great Deliverance

What happens when we direct our attention to God during our trial? We will experience a great deliverance. In David's case, God allowed him to recover all that had been taken by the enemy. While the Lord does not always enable us to recover all of our losses, He does promise to deliver us from all of our afflictions. *"Many are the afflictions of the righteous: but the LORD delivereth him out of them all"* (Psalm 34:19). God may deliver us by removing the problem or by giving grace to sustain us through the trial. Whichever God chooses is best for us, and we will be grateful for His help.

So, what will you do when faced with disappointment in life? Will you get angry and behave irrationally, or will you seek the Lord and experience His divine deliverance? The Lord is waiting to assist you!

"My soul fainteth for thy salvation: but I hope in thy word" –Psalm 119:81.

Day Seven

There's Hope

"Now the God of hope fill you with all joy and peace in believing, that ye may abound in hope, through the power of the Holy Ghost" —Romans 15:13.

How many times have you said, "There's no hope—I'll never be able to get through this"? We all face trials in life that seem absolutely impossible, and we are often tempted to quit when such situations continually bombard us. Have you lost hope today? If so, it's time to claim God's promise of hope! The *"God of hope"* is able to *"fill you with all joy and peace."* In other words, when hope is restored, your joy and peace will be too. Let's consider a couple of ideas about renewing our hope.

We Can Have Hope Continually

Having hope is actually a decision. If you think hope is an emotion, you may wait for a long time until you get a positive feeling. It is better to decide to have hope in God. The psalmist had much trouble, but he chose not to give up. He prayed, *"But I will hope continually, and will yet praise thee more and more"* (Psalm 71:14). Biblical hope does not rely on favorable circumstances. It depends on God, Who is able to change our circumstances. Hope is an expression of faith. Why did the psalmist praise God *"more and more"* in spite of his troubles? Because he knew God would intervene. When your faith is in the Lord, hope does not have to come and go.

Hope Leads to Purity, and a Lack of Hope Leads to Sin

"And every man that hath this hope in him purifieth himself, even as he is pure" (1 John 3:3). Satan does not want you to live a pure life. Therefore, he seeks to discourage you and lead you into hopelessness. Once there, you are ineffective for God and are more likely to sin. Those who lose hope become discouraged, stop trusting God to help them, and turn to sinful vices to escape their problems. For example, someone who becomes depressed may turn to drugs or alcohol to drown their sorrows. Perhaps you have not plunged to those depths but would admit that losing hope has soured your attitude. By renewing your hope in God, you can avoid falling into the traps that Satan has laid for the hopeless.

The Scriptures Give Us Comfort and Hope

You may say, "Well, how do you decide to have hope? It isn't that easy; is it?" It is easy when you follow God's plan. If you want hope from *"the God of hope,"* you must run to His Word and renew your mind. Hopeless people don't think clearly, but those who seek peace from the Scriptures will be comforted and sustained through every trial. Paul said, *"For whatsoever things were written aforetime were written for our learning, that we through patience and comfort of the scriptures might have hope"* (Romans 15:4). When the psalmist faced trouble, he exclaimed, *"My soul fainteth for thy salvation: but I hope in thy word"* (Psalm 119:81). God's Word will give you hope when things are at their worst.

Many years ago, I faced a series of difficult trials that could have easily led to despair. During that time, I began reading in the Psalms every evening to find God's peace and comfort. As David found solace by pouring his heart out to the Lord, I discovered the same thing. My faith and hope were bolstered through extra time in the Word. Because of that experience, I made meditation in the Psalms a part of my routine each evening. God's Word will renew your hope. What steps will you take to strengthen your heart and build hope in the Lord?

Even When There Is No Hope, You Can Still Have Hope

God had promised Abraham that he would be a father of a great nation. However, both he and his wife were too old to have children. Although it was an impossible situation, we read how Abraham decided to have hope. *"Who against hope believed in hope...He staggered not at the promise of God through unbelief; but was strong in faith, giving glory to God"* (Romans 4:18, 20). Notice that Abraham *"believed in hope"* and *"staggered not"* when things were against him. Whatever your problem, you never have to give up. Did giving up ever help you in the past? No! It only led to more problems. So, determine to get comfort and strength from God's Word and trust Him through your trials. With the Lord, there is always hope!

"Thou hast turned for me my mourning into dancing: thou hast put off my sackcloth, and girded me with gladness" -Psalm 30:11.

Day Eight

Blessed Mourning

"Blessed are they that mourn: for they shall be comforted"
—Matthew 5:4.

The words of our text give hope to all who grieve. Not only is a blessing promised to mourners, but the Scripture pronounces the mourner to be blessed. How could this be? The words *blessed* and *mourn* do not seem to go together. To mourn is to grieve, and to be blessed is to be happy. Can one who is grieving possibly be happy? Yes, but he must believe the words spoken by our Lord and apply them to his situation.

The promise makes no mention of the cause of mourning. So, whether our grief is due to unfavorable circumstances or because of our sin, the promise applies. The penitent who grieves over his waywardness and the widow who has been bereaved of her husband can both find solace in their sorrow. How gracious and merciful that the Lord allows those who seek Him to find peace and happiness in times of grief!

Notice that the promised blessing is not something we can only hope for in the distant future. The blessedness that Christ offers is available now. In fact, it has past, present, and future implications.

Past Blessings

First, we have been blessed in the past. If we are currently mourning, that suggests that we have lost something. The fact that we had something to lose means that we were blessed in the first place! Although it may be heart wrenching to suffer the loss of a loved one, it is not meant to be a torturous experience. On one hand we grieve because we miss someone who brought much love and joy to our lives, but on the other hand we rejoice because we were blessed to have enjoyed his or her company and influence for as long as we did. In this way, we are blessed mourners. Though mourning, we are happy for the grace once bestowed upon us. Further, because we have been blessed in the past, we are assured that God will bless us yet again.

Present Blessings

Next, we are presently blessed. The phrase, *"Blessed are they that mourn,"* is in the present tense. A time of mourning does not prevent a state of blessedness. I may be mourning but I am also enjoying God's blessing. It is possible to be presently happy though circumstances are unpleasant. The apostle Paul lost his health, but exclaimed, *"Most gladly therefore will I rather glory in my infirmities, that the power of Christ may rest upon me"* (2 Corinthians 12:9). He spoke of being glad despite his infirmities. Why? Because a blessing accompanied his sorrow—he experienced God's power in his life as a result! By faith, Paul mourned his continual sickness but rejoiced in God's plan for his trial. He was a blessed mourner. Oh, for faith to see the good that God bestows upon us during our seasons of sadness!

Future Blessings

Finally, we will be blessed in the future. I may be grateful for my past blessings and thankful for my present ones, but what will the future hold? The words in our text answer that question. Jesus said that those who mourn *"shall be comforted."* Therefore, I have hope for the future too! Comfort may have left me momentarily, but I am assured that it will soon return. So, I have no need to worry or fear about the heartaches of tomorrow. We will be comforted though we experience a thousand losses. The pain of loss often lingers for a long time, but each recurring pang is relieved by an added blessing from the Lord. His *"compassions fail not. They are new every morning"* (Lamentations 3:22-23).

Conclusion

Allow God's words to cheer your heart today. It is possible to be a blessed mourner. God has pronounced it so already—*"Blessed are they that mourn."* Believe it and find the joy that God wants to give you in your times of sorrow. Don't allow a continual flow of tears to drown a smile from your face.

"Casting all your care upon him; for he careth for you" –1 Peter 5:7.

Day Nine

Anxious Thoughts

"Take therefore no thought for the morrow: for the morrow shall take thought for the things of itself. Sufficient unto the day is the evil thereof" —Matthew 6:34.

Fear and worry grip the hearts of millions of people around the globe. Some people are prone to feeling uneasy, borrowing trouble, and becoming easily overwhelmed. Does that describe you? If you tend to fear the worst in any given situation, you probably have an anxiety problem. Anxiety can affect you physically, emotionally, and spiritually. It can increase your heart rate, affect your breathing, and weaken your body.

According to the Cleveland Clinic, anxiety can be caused by a number of underlying medical conditions.[1] Therefore, it is always wise for people who experience a sudden onset of anxiety problems to consult a doctor. By discovering and treating a hidden medical condition, a person's anxiety problems may begin to clear up.

---

[1] One of the most common medical causes of anxiety is thyroid problems. Other medical considerations that can cause anxiety are infections, vitamin B12 deficiencies, head trauma, brain tumors, electrolyte abnormalities, herbal supplements, large amounts of caffeine, and prescription drugs. (https://health.clevelandclinic.org/is-a-hidden-medical-condition-causing-your-anxiety/), accessed on 9/9/19.

It is important to address anxiety problems because they can impact your relationships with family and friends. Worse than that, they can hinder your fellowship with God. Worry and fear can cripple you spiritually by preventing you from trusting God. Though health care professionals typically attribute anxiety problems to either a medical problem or mental health condition, they tend to overlook spiritual causes and solutions. While medical matters should be treated medically, spiritual ones should be treated Biblically. Not every problem in life requires a pill.

Anxiety is nothing new. People in Jesus' day faced it too. In our text passage, Jesus spoke to people who worried about having their basic needs met. They failed to trust God to feed and clothe them. Such fretting is unnecessary because the Bible is filled with promises about God's provision for His people. As we will see, Jesus gave them spiritual advice and did not provide any medical recommendations. Why? Their problem was obviously a spiritual one. It is not unreasonable, therefore, to conclude that many (not all) anxiety problems stem from spiritual problems. The rest of our discussion, therefore, will focus on the spiritual dimension of fear and worry.

The Characteristics of Anxiety

In Matthew 6:25-34, the word *thought* is used repeatedly. It refers to being full of care or anxious about something. The passage teaches us several characteristics of anxiety.

First, anxiety is common. Jesus mentioned the idea of taking thought (being anxious) five times. To address the issue so many times indicates that it was a common problem among His hearers. Though times have changed, the heart of man hasn't. We all worry at times, and like the people in Christ's day, some in our day are prone to fret and fear far too often. In fact, according to the Anxiety and Depression Association of America, anxiety disorders are listed as the most common mental illness in the U.S.[2] Because the Lord knows that so many struggle with worry and fear, He made a point to address it in the Bible.

Second, anxiety is futile. Notice how useless it is to worry. Jesus asked a simple question—*"Which of you by taking thought* [being anxious] *can add one cubit unto his stature?"* (Matthew 6:27). Can someone make himself taller by worrying about how short he is? No! Some people spend a lot of time worrying about things that they cannot change. The point of Jesus' question was to teach that worry is unprofitable. If you have a problem, becoming anxious will never fix it. God does not want us worrying about things that we cannot change.

Third, anxiety doubts God. We have a faithful Creator. In Matthew 6:26, we see that God feeds the birds, and then we are reminded that we are *"much better than they"* are. Likewise, in verses 28-30, we are told that God arrays the fields with beautiful flowers, and then we are asked, *"shall he not much more clothe you...?"* Christ wanted us to know that we will not be forgotten by our Father. What do you have need of? God knows all about it. Jesus said, *"your heavenly Father knoweth that ye have need of all these things"* (Matthew 6:32). When we worry

---

[2] https://adaa.org/about-adaa/press-room/facts-statistics, accessed on 7/27/19.

about God's provision, we doubt His goodness, integrity, and power. He will take care of us!

Fourth, anxiety borrows trouble. We are instructed, *"Take therefore no thought for the morrow."* In other words, don't be anxious about the future. Anxiety worries about tomorrow and imagines many scenarios that never happen. It brings a pessimistic outlook on life and tends to look for the worst in every situation. Instead of dreaming of tomorrow, anxiety dreads it. If you are prone to worry, you will ruin the present by being fearful of the future. C. H. Spurgeon said, "Anxiety does not empty tomorrow of its sorrows, but only empties today of its strength." Anxiety is a thief. Don't let it into your life, or it will rob you of joy and usefulness.

> Anxiety steals your joy and usefulness.

Fifth, anxiety is sinful. We know that *"whatsoever is not of faith is sin"* (Romans 14:23). Therefore, when anxiety is the result of a lack of faith, it is wrong.[3] Three times in one passage, Jesus commanded us to refrain from being anxious (Matthew 6:25, 31, and 34). Clearly, He told us to stop worrying! Since it is a command, it is sin when we disobey. The Scriptures teach that people can become slaves to sin. Jesus said, *"Whosoever committeth sin is the servant of sin"* (John 8:34). It is possible, therefore, to become enslaved to worry by allowing it to dominate your life. It may be true that some personalities are more prone to being anxious than others, but we should never use that

---

[3] The Scriptures condemn spiritual anxiety which stems from a lack of faith, not medical conditions which can produce anxiety.

as an excuse to worry. Like any other sin, it must be confessed and forsaken. With God's help we can have victory. We will consider that later, but first let's consider why we worry.

The Cause of Anxiety

The main reason for anxiety is a lack faith. When addressing the anxious people in His day, Jesus got to the heart of the matter, saying, *"O ye of little faith"* (Matthew 6:30). Little faith led to big fear. When we stop trusting God to help us, we begin to get uptight and become uneasy. Instead of borrowing trouble, we should have confidence in God. Paul told us that we are to *"walk by faith, not by sight"* (2 Corinthians 5:7). Walking by sight focuses on the problems. It affects our emotions and causes us to become anxious. Walking by faith, however, looks past our problems and sees that the Lord is in control of everything. If you tend to worry, it reveals that you lack faith. Paul mentioned how to cope with affliction—*"While we look not at the things which are seen, but at the things which are not seen: for the things which are seen are temporal; but the things which are not seen are eternal"* (2 Corinthians 4:18). Focus on the eternal God instead of your temporary problems. If circumstances are preventing you from trusting God, stop dwelling on them!

The Cure for Anxiety

Since the cause of anxiety is a lack of faith, the cure is an increase of faith. That is the prescription that Jesus gave. He said, *"But seek ye first the kingdom of God, and his righteousness; and all these things shall be added unto you"* (Matthew 6:33). Faith seeks God instead of dwelling on problems. By seeking the Lord, we build our faith and discover that *"he is a rewarder of them that diligently seek him"* (Hebrews 11:6). Faith believes God despite unfavorable circumstances and secures His peace and blessings. Stop worrying and dreading the worst when a trial enters your life; seek God instead.

We can seek the Lord, not only through prayer, but also by meditating on His Word. Paul taught that the Bible builds faith—*"So then faith cometh by hearing, and hearing by the word of God"* (Romans 10:17). As we saturate our minds with the Word of God and believe it, our faith will increase. When you find yourself becoming anxious, turn to the Bible. God's Word has a way of transforming our thoughts and renewing our minds. That is what Paul meant when he said, *"For which cause we faint not; but though our outward man perish, yet the inward man is renewed day by day"* (2 Corinthians 4:16). Though we may feel overwhelmed at times, the Bible will give us a new outlook.

Conclusion

Nobody is exempt from trials. Though you cannot control what happens to you, you can determine how you respond. Will you become anxious or trust God? If you walk by sight, you cannot walk by faith. Look past your problems and believe that God will take care of you. Being anxious cannot add anything good to your life, but seeking God can—*"all these things shall be added unto you."* Seek Him today!

Day Ten

Rejoicing in Trials

"Wherein ye greatly rejoice, though now for a season, if need be, ye are in heaviness through manifold temptations"
—1 Peter 1:6.

Trials are a part of life. Knowing that does not make them any easier. However, our text gives us hope. Despite *"heaviness"* and *"manifold temptations"* we still have reasons to rejoice.

Rejoice Because Rewards Are Eternal

If your present situation is gloomy, remember the blessings that await you. Peter's exhortation begins, *"Wherein ye greatly rejoice."* The word *wherein* refers back to previous verses that describe our salvation. Why can we *"greatly rejoice"* in the midst of tribulation? Because we have *"an inheritance incorruptible…reserved in heaven"* (1 Peter 1:4). No trouble on earth can deprive us of our heavenly treasures. In fact, trials can actually lead to more rewards in the next life. The apostle Paul reminded us *"that the sufferings of this present time are not worthy to be compared with the glory which shall be revealed in us"* (Romans 8:18). We will be more than duly compensated for our troubles encountered while serving Christ.

Peter gave us even more reason to rejoice, stating that we are *"kept by the power of God"* (1 Peter 1:5). Divine power brings divine protection. Our bodies may be buffeted temporarily by our adversary, but our souls are guarded with a heavenly host that cannot be defeated. Though we sometimes stumble by failing to handle our afflictions properly, our salvation is secure. No lapse of faith will jeopardize our home above. God faithfully keeps us. Let us rejoice that God has kept us and will continue to do so!

The blessings of heaven should become sweeter during our times of affliction. Like thoughts of home comfort a traveler on a long journey, so meditations of heaven sooth our weary souls during this earthly pilgrimage. We can greatly rejoice because we will one day be Home! We must learn to look past our sufferings and see the blessings that await us.

Rejoice Because Trouble Is Limited

Thinking of heaven is great, but it does not take away our immediate problems. Therefore, the Lord gives us hope for the here and now too. Great solace can be found in the reassurance that our burdens are only *"for a season."* Seasons are temporary. In fact, the word *season* refers to a short amount of time. What does this mean to those who are presently troubled? Your problem will one day come to an end! For the Christian, no affliction is

> For the Christian, troubles are not eternal!

eternal. *Manifold temptations* refer to a wide variety of trials that will come and go. Although some trials seem to have no end in sight, they will not last forever. God gives respite in our grief. Heaviness is not meant to be continual but *"for a season."*

When a believer suffers affliction, it is not by random chance. God only permits trouble when He has a purpose for it. The words *"if need be"* are reassuring. The Lord will not allow us to be burdened unnecessarily. He has a reason for every trial that we are called to endure. Though Joseph was abused by his brethren, sold into slavery, falsely accused, imprisoned wrongfully, and forgotten by one he had helped, God had not forgotten him. The Lord had a purpose for each difficulty Joseph experienced. In the end, God promoted Joseph to be the second most powerful man on earth and used him to save multitudes from famine. Rather than become bitter because of his trouble, he proclaimed, *"God meant it unto good"* (Genesis 50:20). As Joseph realized that God's plan was best, so will you if you trust Him.

Paul was a man who suffered greatly for the cause of Christ, yet he maintained a joyful spirit. How? He saw his trials through the eye of faith. His words of exhortation echo those of Peter. Paul testified that *"our light affliction, which is but for a moment, worketh for us a far more exceeding and eternal weight of glory"* (2 Corinthians 4:17). Let us rejoice that our troubles on earth are limited and our rewards in heaven are abundant! Never let waves of affliction dampen your spirit. Instead, *"greatly rejoice."*

"He raiseth up the poor out of the dust, and lifteth the needy out of the dunghill"
-Psalm 113:7.

Day Eleven

The Way Up Is Down

"The LORD maketh poor, and maketh rich: he bringeth low, and lifteth up" —1 Samuel 2:7.

When life takes a downward turn, it is an unpleasant experience. Let's face it—*down* usually has negative connotations. We do not like it when our health or wealth goes down. At work, we hope for a promotion, not a demotion. Investors dread entering an economic downturn. We certainly don't like to hear that our car is broken down. Even when describing our feelings, we reserve the phrase "I'm feeling down" to refer to a time of discouragement. If the circumstances of life have gotten you down, it's time to look up. That's what Hannah did. She took her burden to the Lord and poured her heart out in prayer. The Lord answered her request and filled her heart with joy. The words of our text were spoken by Hannah as a testimony of what God can do for all who are downhearted—*"he bringeth low, and lifteth up."* As He changed her condition, He can change ours too!

A Promising Principle

It is true that life is filled with ups and downs. However, what we typically fail to see is that God intends to use our down times to prepare us for something better. In God's economy, the way up is down.

Our text reminds us the order in which God often works—*"The LORD maketh poor, and maketh rich: he bringeth low, and lifteth up."* He allows us to suffer hardships before showering us with blessings. The first part of this promise is an encouragement for all who face financial difficulties. If we are poor now, God may soon increase our riches. The apostle Paul testified, *"I know both how to be abased, and I know how to abound"* (Philippians 4:12). He had learned to be content with little, and that prepared him to be able to handle much. Those who have risen to prosperity from poverty tend to appreciate their belongings more than those who were born with a silver spoon in their mouth. The point is that times of poorness prepare us to be more thankful in times of plenty. Let us be content with our little, knowing that the Lord will bless with more when the timing is right.

Our text not only addresses material needs but also speaks to those who have been cast down. *"The LORD…bringeth low, and lifteth up."* Notice that God's order is often lowering before lifting. The psalmist testified, *"The LORD preserveth the simple: I was brought low, and he helped me"* (Psalm 116:6). Before he could be lifted up, he had to be *"brought low."* Demotion often precedes promotion. C. H. Spurgeon said, "It is the method of his grace to humble those whom he means to exalt. None will ever be rich in Christ until they are made to feel that they are bankrupt in

> Today's troubles pave the way for tomorrow's blessings.

themselves." If we must be humbled in order to reach new heights with Christ, we cheerfully accept God's plan.

An Encouraging Example

God often allows His children to suffer loss before blessing them. Was it not that way for Job? He lost his children, his wealth, and his health. In the end, we read, *"...the LORD gave Job twice as much as he had before"* (Job 42:10). We tend to focus on the present, making it difficult to look toward the future. However, we must remember that much of what happens in our present circumstances plays a role in our future. While we are more concerned about now, God is more concerned about hereafter. Though Job had to endure great hardships, the Lord had a plan for his future. *"Behold, we count them happy which endure. Ye have heard of the patience of Job, and have seen the end of the Lord; that the Lord is very pitiful, and of tender mercy"* (James 5:11). As Job needed patience to see *"the end"* result of God's plan, so do we. What might appear to be burdensome to us presently will be seen as a blessing later. Surely, like Job, we will be *"happy"* if we *"endure."*

A Heavenly Healing

At times, the Lord humbles our haughty spirits through chastening. His intent is not to harm us but to help us. When He inflicts pain, it is only because He plans to relieve it. His goal is to turn us back to Himself. The prophet said, *"Come, and let us return unto the LORD: for he hath torn, and he will heal us; he hath smitten, and he will bind us up"* (Hosea 6:1). Have you strayed from the Lord? If so, God's smiting hand is ready to heal. What is required is that you first *"return unto the LORD."* God may bring us low through chastening, but it is only so He can restore us to good spiritual health. Once again, we see that God's order is *down* before *up*.

Conclusion

We have learned that those whom God chooses to fill, He must first empty, and the ones He chooses to exalt, He will first humble. Today's troubles pave the way for tomorrow's blessings. Hardships precede betterment. This is how God works, and we are happy it is so. Otherwise, we would not appreciate God's lovingkindness nearly as much had we not experienced difficulty or deprivation. If God has decided that the way up is down, then we would not choose a shortcut to the mountaintop without first passing through the valley. Let us remember to look at troubles as opportunities for the Lord to help. Too often we look at the negative side of things and forget that God plans to bring good out of our disappointments. If you are presently down, wait for God to lift you up. Like David, you will soon be able to proclaim, *"He brought me up also out of an horrible pit, out of the miry clay, and set my feet upon a rock, and established my goings"* (Psalm 40:2). Hallelujah!

Day Twelve

The Day of Trouble

"Offer unto God thanksgiving; and pay thy vows unto the most High: And call upon me in the day of trouble: I will deliver thee, and thou shalt glorify me"
—Psalm 50:14-15.

Life is not always easy. Instead of triumph, sometimes we have trouble. Our text speaks of *"the day of trouble."* Perhaps today is such a day for you. When our problems are small, we don't tend to worry too much, but when they are frequent or overwhelming, we can become greatly distressed. Thankfully, God has shown us in His Word what we should do when we face the day of trouble. Let's consider some wonderful truths from the passage above.

The Preparation

Before God mentioned the day of trouble in verse 15, He told us how we can prepare for it in verse 14. We are exhorted, *"Offer unto God thanksgiving; and pay thy vows unto the most High."* Two things are mentioned here that will help us to be in a right spiritual condition when trials enter our lives.

First, we should maintain an attitude of praise—*"Offer unto God thanksgiving."* A heart filled with gratitude magnifies the Lord. When our focus is upon how great He is, the problems of this world do not seem as big. Too often, however, our hearts are not in tune with the Lord, and when trouble comes, we do not react properly. If you find yourself getting irritated, angry, or discouraged because of problems, it usually means that your heart was not right before the day of trouble arrived.

Second, we should keep our promises—*"pay thy vows unto the most High."* Have you made any promises to God? Notice to whom you promised—*"the most High."* By respecting and honoring Him on a daily basis, we have greater confidence in turning to Him when we have problems. If you disregard and disobey God, you will discover that *"your sins have hid his face from you"* (Isaiah 59:2). When the day of trouble comes, we do not want to be far from the Lord. Therefore, by living right, we will stay close to our great Deliverer!

The Problem

Now that we have seen how we can prepare for the day of trouble, let us consider what such a day might be like. It might be a day of health trouble, financial trouble, family trouble, neighbor trouble, work trouble, car trouble, or emotional trouble. The word *trouble* can refer to affliction, annoyance, adversity, anguish, distress, disturbance, or tribulation. None of those words sound pleasant. Even the description of the word *trouble* is troubling!

While serving as a missionary in Zambia, a young girl named Mapenzi attended our church. The name Mapenzi means "trouble." I used to tease her and say, "Here comes Trouble!" or "Every time you come to church we have Trouble." Although we would have fun with her name, trouble is often no laughing matter. It can be heartbreaking and devastating at times. Over the years, I have ministered to women who lost their husbands and children who became orphans. Losing a loved one, facing a life-threatening illness, or experiencing a financial crisis can weigh heavily upon any of us. Regardless of what trials we face, we should not worry because God has told us what to do when trouble comes.

The Prescription

The Lord has prescribed a simple treatment for all of our troubles, whether they are great or small. He said, *"...call upon me in the day of trouble."* Real trouble must be met with real faith in a real God through real prayer. When it is, real answers follow. When Hannah was overwhelmed, she got serious about praying and testified, *"I...have poured out my soul before the LORD"* (1 Samuel 1:15). God saw her affliction, heard her prayer, and granted her request. Heartfelt prayers like Hannah's get the Lord's attention and secure His help. Too often, our prayers lack faith and fervency. David exhorts us to pray in a similar manner as Hannah, saying, *"Trust in him at all times; ye people, pour out your heart before him: God is a refuge for us"* (Psalm 62:8). Let's face it; some of our prayers are more pitiful than powerful because our requests are not urgent. Though we may not like trouble, it certainly helps our prayer life become more focused and fruitful.

God's prescription is, *"call upon me in the day of trouble."* Notice that the *"me"* in the verse is *"the most High."* We have the privilege to take our problems directly to the Ruler of the universe. We are encouraged, *"Let us therefore come boldly unto the throne of grace, that we may obtain mercy, and find grace to help in time of need"* (Hebrew 4:16). Since He is the Most High, He is able to help, and since He is merciful, He is willing to do so. As Creator, no law of nature or scheme of man can hinder Him. The psalmist proclaimed, *"God is our refuge and strength, a very present help in trouble"* (Psalm 46:1). Being *"very present"* assures us that God is right beside us and ready to intervene. If we follow His prescription and call upon Him, we will soon see Him at work on our behalf.

The Promise

Not only did the Lord tell us what to do in our day of trouble, He also told us what He would do. When we call upon Him, He promised, *"I will deliver thee."* The word *deliver* in this passage means "to loose, to pull off, to take away." When God delivers us, He loosens the grip that our trouble has on us. He might not always take away our troubles, but He can take us away from them. By calling on God, our attention is removed from our problems and placed where it should be—on the Lord. When that happens, we are delivered from the torment associated with our problems. Casting our burdens upon the Lord brings great relief! Let's analyze God's promise one word at a time. *I* (this refers to Almighty God Who makes impossibilities possible) *will* (that is a certainty, leaving no doubt at all) *deliver* (this involves either taking us away from the problem or loosening the grip that the problem has on us) *thee* (that means you, not just everybody else). The promise of deliverance is for you. Believe it and claim it today.

The Purpose

Why does God allow *"the day of trouble"*? Notice His purpose—*"thou shalt glorify me."* Here's how God's plan works: He permits trouble in our lives, we draw close to Him, He delivers, and we glorify Him. Our troubles allow us to see God's power at work that we wouldn't see otherwise. Without troubling times, we would not experience divine deliverance. Have you not seen God deliver you in the past and praised Him for it? Was it not a glorious day when you saw God personally work on your behalf? Can He not bless you in such a way again?

Conclusion

Help in the day of trouble causes us to realize how good God is to us and leads us to praise Him more as a result. At the end of the psalm we have been studying, we read, *"Whoso offereth praise glorifieth me: and to him that ordereth his conversation aright will I shew the salvation of God"* (Psalm 50:23). Trouble leads to prayer, prayer leads to deliverance, deliverance leads to praise, and praise glorifies our wonderful Lord. Therefore, we will not fear the day of trouble, knowing that our Lord will be exalted more because of it. After all, our lives *"were created by him, and for him"* (Colossians 1:16). Lord, we know that You have a plan for our trouble, and we praise You for it.

"Peace I leave with you, my peace I give unto you: not as the world giveth, give I unto you. Let not your heart be troubled, neither let it be afraid" -John 14:27.

Day Thirteen

God's Exchange Program

"The Spirit of the Lord GOD is upon me...to appoint unto them that mourn in Zion, to give unto them beauty for ashes, the oil of joy for mourning, the garment of praise for the spirit of heaviness" —Isaiah 61:1, 3.

The above passage speaks of the tender mercies that God will extend to the Jews who will suffer terribly during the Tribulation. The Lord promised not only to remove their grief, but to replace it with things far better! It is God's exchange program. Notice how it works—He gives *"beauty for ashes, the oil of joy for mourning, the garment of praise for the spirit of heaviness."* He is ready to cheer the mourning soul! Is your heart heavy today? If so, allow the Lord to brighten your outlook with His goodness.

Though this promise is given to restored Israel, by faith we can appropriate the same blessings. We know that since God gave His Son, He will not withhold lesser gifts. The teaching of the apostle Paul bears this out. He said, *"He that spared not his own Son, but delivered him up for us all, how shall he not with him also freely give us all things?"* (Romans 8:32). Knowing that the promise is for us, let us enjoy its benefits.

Before going any further, we must remember who the *"me"* is in our text. This is none other than the Lord Jesus. We take great comfort in knowing that our Savior sees our affliction and has a remedy for *"them that mourn."* Of course, this also serves as a gentle reminder that even those whom the Lord loves will have times of mourning. Did not many of God's faithful servants pass through seasons of deep sorrow?

Thankfully, Christ runs to our aid with a healing balm for our souls. His great sufferings prepared Him to enter into our sorrows and empathize with us. The writer of Hebrews reinforced this idea, saying, *"For in that he himself hath suffered being tempted, he is able to succour them that are tempted"* (Hebrews 2:18). There is not a sorrow that He has not experienced. He is *"a man of sorrows, and acquainted with grief"* (Isaiah 53:3). Whatever your heartache, He is the only One Who truly knows how you feel. Further, nobody loves you as much as He does. Has He ever refused to comfort the brokenhearted? No! Never forget that He came to *"to bind up the brokenhearted"* (Isaiah 61:1).

> Christ's hurt prepared Him to help.

We will all face seasons of mourning, but Jesus will rush to our side and offer grace for our grief. In every case of sorrow, God has promised to replace our sadness with a blessing. Has not experience already proven that God's exchange program is able to transform us? At salvation, Christ replaced our sin with His righteousness. He removed our guilt and made us innocent in His sight. Let us be assured that He will not stop there. He is willing to comfort all who mourn. Let those who are downhearted request relief for their grief.

We may have to wait for His providence to work out the timing, but solace will come in the end. The only thing that will hinder us from receiving it is a lack of faith. Are you ready to trust Jesus to change your disposition? He will give to those who mourn *"beauty for ashes, the oil of joy for mourning, the garment of praise for the spirit of heaviness."* Hallelujah!

Now that we are assured that the promise is ours and that the Prince of Peace Himself will deliver it, let us determine to get involved in God's exchange program. Our next three devotional readings will consider what awaits us in greater detail.

"And let the beauty of the LORD our God be upon us: and establish thou the work of our hands upon us; yea, the work of our hands establish thou it" -Psalm 90:17.

Day Fourteen

Beauty for Ashes

"To appoint unto them that mourn…beauty for ashes"
—Isaiah 61:3.

The words *"beauty for ashes"* provide hope for all who are downhearted. They are the first part of God's exchange program. When we give Him our ashes, He replaces them with beauty. Could we expect anything less from our great God? First, we will consider our ashes and then we will discuss His promised beautification.

Our Ashes

Ashes speak of loss. When something is consumed, all that remains is residue of its former state. The gray color of ash lends to gloominess. Its frail composition and light weight leave us with just enough to remind us of our loss but not enough of it to enjoy. Are you grieving because of loss in your life? Losing a loved one, health, or financial stability can lead to discouragement. The person or treasure that has been dear to your heart will be terribly missed, but you must not remain focused on your loss indefinitely. You must look ahead to the beauty that God promises to bestow upon you. He promises to change your disposition, turning a frown into a smile. It may be hard to believe that you can be happy again, but God promises to give a countenance that radiates with beauty.

Ashes symbolize sorrow. Perhaps you recall reading in the Scriptures of mourners who covered themselves in sackcloth and ashes. Why would they adorn themselves in such an unbecoming manner? It was an outward expression of an inner feeling of grief. Though such a custom is not practiced in our culture, we find ways to express our grief. Some put on a long face, others slump in their posture, and not a few wear their feelings on their sleeves. When people display their discouragement, hopelessness, or irritability, it is often a way to tell others, "Hey, I'm hurting." What they fail to realize is that wearing their ashes is not attractive to others. In many cases, we drive people away when we dab on the ashes. At times, we are happy to be left alone so we can sit and sulk, but isolation does not bring relief. Wallowing in ashes has never made anybody beautiful. There is, however, hope. Jesus promised to give *"beauty for ashes."* Oh, how that should cause us to shout for joy!

Ashes represent repentance. In Biblical times, ashes were often worn to show humility and sorrow for sin. Though Job handled his great loss well initially, he took his eyes off the Lord and focused on his troubles. Thus, he allowed his sorrow to sour his attitude. After the Lord rebuked him, he cried out, *"Wherefore I abhor myself, and repent in dust and ashes"* (Job 42:6). Have you allowed your grief to sever your fellowship with God? If so, it may be time to *"repent in dust and ashes."* Tell the Lord that you are sorry for allowing your problems to cause you to doubt His love and faithfulness. Acknowledge that He knows what is best and that *"all things work together for* *good to them that love God, to them who are the called according to his purpose"* (Romans 8:28).

Perhaps your sin is worse than Job's. His sorrow began, not because of outward rebellion, but by failing to trust God in his time of affliction. Many people enter a season of sadness because of sowing seeds of iniquity. The prophet Hosea described the fate of such individuals, *"For they have sown the wind, and they shall reap the whirlwind"* (Hosea 8:7). Many have discovered the hard way that sin brings misery, not happiness. If this is your case, it is time to put on the ashes of repentance. All

> Seeds of sinfulness yield seasons of sadness.

who do will experience God's mercy and forgiveness. As the prodigal's father ran to meet him and arrayed him with the best robe, our heavenly Father offers us *"beauty for ashes."* The Lord delights in restoring wayward children. Whether you have strayed from Him outwardly like the prodigal or inwardly like Job, return to the Lord and allow Him to make your life beautiful once again.

We have dwelt on the despondency of ashes long enough. Now, let us turn our attention to the promised replacement.

God's Beauty

Beauty is lost as a result of sin. David prayed, *"When thou with rebukes dost correct man for iniquity, thou makest his beauty to consume away like a moth"* (Psalm 39:11). He acknowledged that as righteousness beautifies the inner man, sin mars the soul. The Lord will allow us to suffer loss, but His intention is to draw us closer to

Himself. Unfortunately, we often lose hope instead of trusting *"the God of hope"* (Romans 15:13). When we set our eyes upon our sorrows, our inner beauty is tarnished, and this is a direct result of God's chastening hand. Though He wants to bless us during our times of sadness, He cannot put His stamp of approval on our lack of faith. However, once we renew our faith, our beauty is restored. If you have suffered loss as a result of sin, you will find your beauty return after you have returned to the Lord. Examine your heart for any known sin, and confess it at once. Soon, your ashes will be replaced!

Beauty is a bonus blessing. For the Lord to remove the ashes from our darkened countenances would be enough of a blessing. However, He takes it a step further and adds His charm. To get a mental picture, think of a filthy, impoverished little girl who is taken under the wing of a kind family. She is bathed in sweet-smelling suds, adorned with a pretty dress, and given a cute little bow for her hair. Though a bath would be a blessing, the extras make her the most cheerful little girl in town. That is how God wants to treat us! Truly, *"where sin abounded, grace did much more abound"* (Romans 5:20). Praise God for His abounding grace!

Beauty speaks of holiness. David encouraged his fellow believers to *"worship the LORD in the beauty of holiness"* (Psalm 29:2). When God gives us beauty, it is in the form of righteousness. In fact, our text verse bears this out. Notice after promising *"beauty for ashes,"* God elaborates on His purpose for doing so. He said, *"that they might be called trees of righteousness, the planting of the LORD, that he might be glorified"* (Isaiah 61:3). If you long to be more like the Savior and bring glory to His name, you are a prime candidate to receive the beauty of righteousness. Trees are stately and stunning when they are full, lush, and blooming. Oh, to be planted by the Lord and flourish as a strong fruitful tree! Lord, take my ashes of distrust and faithlessness and replace them with *"the beauty of holiness."*

Beauty brings confidence. Is there not an extra bounce in our step when we are feeling clean and spiffy? Solomon said, *"In the fear of the LORD is strong confidence"* (Proverbs 14:26). When we walk uprightly in the fear of God, our prayer life will take on new boldness. No longer will we wallow in self-pity over our troubles, but we will be assured that God is working on our behalf. Furthermore, our service and witness for Christ will be sprinkled with renewed expectation. When feeling down and dejected, our confidence is low. It is time to exchange your ashes for God's fortifying beauty.

Beauty attracts others. The purpose of our beautification is not to draw attention to ourselves. Such a proud attitude is repulsive to God, not attractive. Certainly, with Christ's righteousness, the Lord will have more delight in us. However, He intends that our comeliness would be the means to charm others to Himself. We are each an epistle, *"known and read of all men"* (2 Corinthians 3:2). If our countenances are disfigured by continual sorrow, we will attract very few to the Lord. When He replaces our ashes with His beauty, we become a trophy of His grace and mercy. Never allow your grief and darkness to cast a shadow on the

> Wallowing in ashes does little to attract men to Christ.

goodness of God. He wants to make you a blessing to others.

Conclusion

Have you been wearing the ashes of loss, sorrow, or repentance? If so, God promises to give you *"beauty for ashes."* He wants you to shine for Him! When your ashes are replaced by His beautification, your hope and confidence will be restored. So, go ahead and ask the Lord to exchange your gloomy ashen countenance with a beautiful, radiant smile. Once your inner man is renewed, your entire demeanor will change!

Day Fifteen

The Oil of Joy

"To appoint unto them that mourn...the oil of joy for mourning"—Isaiah 61:3.

We have already seen that the Lord delights to give *"beauty for ashes."* Now we will consider the next part of God's Exchange Program—*"the oil of joy for mourning."*

Ashes are the outward expression of grief, and mourning is the inward reality. It is wonderful that the Lord provides a remedy for the external problem, appointing *"beauty for ashes."* However, what we need is an inner cure, not only an external beautification. Thankfully, the Lord treats the whole man. By creating inner joy, our outward appearance is mended. Solomon put it this way, *"A merry heart maketh a cheerful countenance"* (Proverbs 15:13). The *"oil of joy"* is the remedy that cheers the heart.

It is interesting that the Lord used the phrase *"oil of joy"* instead of simply saying *"joy."* This indicates that there is something special about oil that produces joy. By considering some of the uses of oil in Scripture, we better understand how it produces joy in the life of a believer.

Oil Heals

The parable of the Good Samaritan reminds us of the medicinal qualities of oil. The Samaritan moved to help the injured man. Notice that as he *"bound up his wounds,"* he was also *"pouring in oil and wine"* (Luke 10:34). The wine served as an antiseptic, and the oil soothed the wound. The oil aided the healing process and provided comfort.

Do you have a wounded heart? Will not our Savior pour in *"the oil of joy"* to soothe your sorrowful soul? Is He not able to comfort your broken spirit? We cannot expect the Good Shepherd to be less sympathetic than the Good Samaritan! As the Samaritan brought healing to the battered man, Christ will do the same for all who have experienced pain, sorrow, or abuse. Never forget the healing power of joy. It heals the heart as oil comforts and mends the body. If you are feeling down today, what you need is a healthy dose of joy. Ask the Lord to replace your mourning with joy.

> The oil of joy is God's remedy for hurting hearts.

Oil Empowers

Just two verses prior to the phrase *"the oil of joy,"* we discover that this anointing refers to the Spirit of God—*"The Spirit of the Lord GOD is upon me; because the LORD hath anointed me"* (Isaiah 61:1). Oil symbolizes the Holy Spirit. When we are anointed with the Holy Spirit, we find power to overcome sorrow. The believers in Thessalonica provide an astounding example of this. Their trouble did not rob them of their happiness. Despite *"much affliction"* they had *"joy of the Holy Ghost"* (1 Thessalonians 1:6). Why? Because they *"received the word"* (1 Thessalonians 1:6). There is a connection between joy and the Bible. The Spirit of God uses the Word of God to bring the joy of God. Never let your sorrow prevent you from seeking comfort from the Scriptures. The Bible is not only the Sword of the Spirit, it is also the lamp which He uses to brighten our path and warm our hearts.

Oftentimes when people experience great sorrow and heartache, they focus on changing their circumstances. However, we cannot always control our circumstances. If we have joy only when all is well, it is not true joy. The only way to have lasting joy is through the power of the Holy Spirit. When He anoints us, we can have joy even in times of *"much affliction."*

Oil Protects

Sorrow affects our minds. Too often, discouraged people entertain harmful thoughts. When relief is not found, the pain and agony of a broken heart can become almost unbearable. What is needed is something that will protect the mind from self-destructive thinking.

We turn to the beloved 23rd Psalm for another purpose for oil—protection. We are familiar with the line, *"thou anointest my head with oil"* (Psalm 23:5). In his classic book, *A Shepherd Looks at Psalm 23,* Phillip Keller described how flies created a lot of trouble for his sheep. Their larvae would travel up a sheep's nose, causing inflammation and pain. Sheep would become so irritable that they would injure themselves by thrashing their heads violently. All they focused on was immediate relief, and of course their aggravation only made matters worse. To protect the sheep from such trouble, shepherds anointed the heads of their sheep with oil to keep the flies away.

The picture for us is clear. Our heads must be protected from the troubling pests of fear, anxiety, and discouragement. Without an anointing from the Good Shepherd, people allow wrong thoughts to enter their minds. Then, in a frenzy to find relief, they stop thinking rationally and create more pain for themselves by acting foolishly.

> The oil of joy relieves the troubled mind.

Have you allowed your sorrow to lead to frustration and anxiousness? If so, it is time to exchange your mourning for *"the oil of joy."* Ask the Good Shepherd for His mind-protecting joy. Keller said, "Once the oil had been applied to the sheep's head there was an immediate change in behavior. Gone was the aggravation; gone the frenzy; gone the irritability and the restlessness."[4] A dose of God's protecting oil will bring instantaneous relief. Receive *"the oil of joy"* at once! Focusing on your hurts will only allow Satan's parasites of despair and depression to further annoy your mind.

Immediately following David's declaration that his head was anointed with oil, he announced, *"my cup runneth over."* David was overwhelmed with joy because of God's anointing oil. The Good Shepherd will relieve and protect your mind, too, if you ask Him.

---

[1] Phillip Keller, *A Shepherd Looks at Psalm 23* (Grand Rapids: Zondervan, 1970), 113.

Conclusion

Mourning can lead to a host of detrimental effects on the body and soul. Rather than continue in our sorrow, we can accept the Lord's offer to replace our grief with joy. In particular, we are promised *"the oil of joy for mourning."* Using the symbol of oil, we see that God's joy heals our broken hearts, empowers us to rise above our afflictions, and protects our minds from harmful thoughts.

Are you feeling too weak to anoint yourself with this precious oil? Do not worry. Ask the Lord to do for you what you cannot do for yourself. It is the job of the Good Shepherd to anoint His sheep's heads with oil.

Let us not lose focus of the Giver of this grand gift of joy. Jesus is the One Who turns sorrow into smiles. Let us pursue Him more than we seek His blessings. If we have Him, we have all that He offers. If your relationship with the Savior has grown cold, renew it at once! He is ready to give you *"the oil of joy for mourning."*

"The LORD is my strength and my shield; my heart trusted in him, and I am helped: therefore my heart greatly rejoiceth; and with my song will I praise him" -Psalm 28:7.

Day Sixteen

The Garment of Praise

"To appoint unto them that mourn…the garment of praise for the spirit of heaviness" —Isaiah 61:3.

Garments are often chosen to express how we feel. If your garments were to express the current condition of your heart, would your clothes be bright and festive or dark and dreary? The spirit of heaviness, though an inner problem, often has visible manifestations.

The Lord provides hope for all who are suffering from heaviness. He promises to exchange a darkened spirit with a bright new outlook. Instead of continuing to strike a minor key, you can sing joyfully. Claim the promise that God so graciously offers in today's text—*"the garment of praise for the spirit of heaviness."*

The Spirit of Heaviness

How can a heavy heart be described? Two words quickly come to mind: discouragement and darkness. First, notice that those with heavy hearts are discouraged. Solomon aptly stated, *"Heaviness in the heart of man maketh it stoop"* (Proverbs 12:25). Have you allowed your heart to be weighed down with sorrow, causing you to mope? A heavy heart will make you feel like doing little for

God and others. Second, people with heavy hearts are darkened. The word *heaviness* in our text implies dimness and darkness. What is needed is something to brighten our spirits. What could be better than putting on the garment of praise? Praise drives away darkness. It turns our focus from self to God. Our hearts are clouded with sin and sorrow, but Jesus provides light and life. We can be delivered from the spirit of heaviness.

What causes a heavy heart? Heaviness can be caused by either sin or circumstance. David testified how sin weighed him down, saying, *"For mine iniquities are gone over mine head: as an heavy burden they are too heavy for me"* (Psalm 38:4). Sin is a burden that is *"too heavy"* for us to carry. Unconfessed sin is the source of many heartaches and must be forsaken. Circumstances often contribute to a heavy heart. Disappointments of life can pile up and weigh us down. The psalmist cried out, *"My soul melteth for heaviness"* (Psalm 119:28). When something melts, it is weak and unstable. If we do not handle our trials properly, our hearts will weaken.

What is the cure for a heavy heart? Whether heaviness is caused by sin or circumstance, though the root may be different, the remedy is the same. By faith, we must turn to the Savior. He alone can forgive our sins and fortify our souls. The One Who promised to remove your *"spirit of heaviness"* can do so because He has already carried the load. *"Surely he hath borne our griefs, and carried our sorrows"* (Isaiah 53:4). There is no need for you to carry the burden that He has already shouldered. When Jesus prayed in the Garden of

> Why carry a burden that Christ is willing to carry for you?

Gethsemane, He was *"sorrowful and very heavy"* (Matthew 26:37). He carried a greater burden than we will ever face. Since He is well acquainted with grief, He is sympathetic to our plight and willing to help us.

If you have sins that have weighed you down, confess them at once. A cleansed heart will give you something to sing about! If your heaviness is from unfavorable circumstances, follow David's advice—*"Cast thy burden upon the LORD, and he shall sustain thee"* (Psalm 55:22). When you give your trouble to God, He will carry it for you. The Lord can lighten your load!

The Garment of Praise

After God replaces our sorrow with joy, what should follow? Praise! When our inner sackcloth of heaviness is removed, our outer garb will change too. No longer will we be pouting but praising. God promises to swap *"the garment of praise for the spirit of heaviness."* The tongue that is bound in the dungeon of discouragement can be loosed to sing the Savior's praises. Notice some things that garments do for a person.

Garments cover us. After Jesus cast the demons out of the maniac in Gadara, the man was found with Jesus in a new condition—he was *"sitting, and clothed, and in his right mind"* (Mark 5:15). One of the first things we notice about the man was that he was clothed. His sin and shame were covered, and his new clothing was symbolic of being covered with Christ's righteousness. The change of body, soul, and spirit even affected his lips. Notice that he *"began to publish...how great things Jesus had done for him"* (Mark 5:20). In like manner, the garment of praise should completely cover our feeble hearts. When it does, thanksgiving will gush from our lips as waters sprang from the rock which Moses struck in the wilderness. Allow praise to flow as a continual stream, not like an occasional drip from a leaky faucet. Are you clothed in the garment of praise? If not, do not hesitate to take Christ at His word and exchange your heavy heart for a joyous one.

Garments protect us. Though David despaired for his life at times, he learned that prayer and praise to God brought great deliverance. He testified, *"I will call upon the LORD, who is worthy to be praised: so shall I be saved from mine enemies"* (Psalm 18:3). His confidence in God was a result of his faith, and his faith was demonstrated by his praise. As a garment protects our bodies, so praise protects our hearts. Do not allow a heavy heart to rob you of the protective power that the garment of praise offers.

Garments cheer us. Some clothing makes us happy. Certain colors, patterns, and designs bring pleasure. David described the joy that came to his heart when God lifted his heavy burden and replaced it with the garment of praise. Consider his prayer to God, *"Thou hast turned for me my mourning into dancing: thou hast put off my sackcloth, and girded me with gladness"* (Psalm 30:11). Do you long to be *"girded...with gladness"*? Ask the Lord to remove your *"spirit of heaviness"* and replace it with *"the garment of praise."* How happy you will be when God changes your vestments!

Garments identify us. When the father of the prodigal wanted to show affection to his repentant son, he gave him new clothing. He commanded, *"Bring forth the best robe, and put it on him; and put a ring on his hand, and shoes on his feet"* (Luke 15:22). He could not bear to see his son dressed in beggarly rags. In like manner, our heavenly Father desires to adorn us with beautiful garments of praise to replace our tattered hearts of heaviness. When our Father gives us *"the best robe,"* it shows the world to Whom we belong, and He is glorified for the changes He makes in our lives. He longs to bless us in such a manner for His name's sake. When our mouths are filled with praise to the Lord, there is no doubt we belong to Christ. Do not think for a moment that God would withhold the garment of praise from you. It would bring dishonor to His name. If you are a Christian, you belong to Him, and He will provide you with a fitting covering to reflect His goodness to your fellow man.

Garments warm us. What a winter coat does for the body, praise does for the soul. If you are feeling the chill of despondency, wrap yourself with praise. Nothing can drive away the draft of despair like the garment of gratitude. In a psalm of praise, David uttered these words, *"Make thy face to shine upon thy servant"* (Psalm 31:16). His praise gave confidence that the Lord would shine upon him and warm his heart. Oh that our praise would bring warmth to our souls too!

Conclusion

Do you have ashes? Bring them to the Lord and receive beauty. Are you in mourning? Remind God that He promised the oil of joy. Is a spirit of heaviness upon you? Cast it off and be clad with the garment of praise.

"I will never leave thee, nor forsake thee"
-Hebrews 13:5.

Day Seventeen

Never Alone

"I will not leave you comfortless: I will come to you"
—John 14:18.

Are you lonely? You do not have to be. Loneliness occurs when we are without a friend or companion. For those who know Christ as Savior, they have *"a friend that sticketh closer than a brother"* (Proverbs 18:24). Though other friends may abandon us, the Lord promised, *"I will never leave thee, nor forsake thee"* (Hebrews 13:5). If you are a Christian, you are never alone!

Unfortunately, there are times that we feel alone. Why? Perhaps we have neglected His presence. Since He never leaves us, we should never be overcome with loneliness. However, at times we begin to feel sorry for ourselves and indulge in pity parties. As strange as it sounds, we often want to be alone when we wallow in self-pity. While the pity party is in full swing, we may want to invite others to it, but we plan on doing all the talking. Jesus sees when things are not well in your life, and it is His desire to draw near and console you. He promised, *"I will not leave you comfortless: I will come to you"* (John 14:18). If you are lonely, all you need to do is acknowledge the One Who is trying to engage your fellowship.

It is true that losing a loved one leaves a huge void in one's life. Grief is normal, but once again it is meant to turn our attention to the Lord and strengthen our relationship with Him. Having a broken heart is understandable, but don't forget that the Savior wants to mend it. He said, *"The Spirit of the Lord is upon me…he hath sent me to heal the brokenhearted"* (Luke 4:18). Allow Him to do His job of healing!

When we are bereaved of loved ones, God steps in and extends special care to us. The psalmist said, *"When my father and my mother forsake me, then the LORD will take me up"* (Psalm 27:10). Regardless of who we lose, we must focus on what we gain. Who could comfort and cheer us better than the Lord? If you are sad and lonely, turn at once to the waiting Savior and enjoy the sweetness of His counsel, the gentle touch of His Spirit, and the reassurance of His constant love. Open your Bible and allow Him to settle your fears and fill your lonely heart with hope. The psalmist found God's Word to be a source of strength and encouragement. He offered these words of praise, *"Thou art my hiding place and my shield: I hope in thy word"* (Psalm 119:114). Will you allow God to fill your heart with hope through His Word?

> In every loss, learn to think upon what you gain.

Loneliness is a self-inflicted emotion for the Christian because he has God's abiding presence. When David found himself feeling lonely, he sought the Lord. He prayed, *"Turn thee unto me, and have mercy upon me; for I am desolate and afflicted"* (Psalm 25:16). Allow each pang of loneliness to trigger a prayer similar to David's. Soon, you will have the same comfort he enjoyed.

Jesus faced times when He was alone. Shortly before His crucifixion He spoke to the disciples, *"ye shall be scattered, every man to his own, and shall leave me alone: and yet I am not alone, because the Father is with me"* (John 16:32). Though He was forsaken by earthly friends, He understood that as long as He had the Father, He was not alone. Then, the most horrible thing happened to Him. When the sins of the world were placed upon Him, the Father forsook Him. He was totally alone. Because of His sacrifice, no Christian will ever experience the loss of the Father's presence like He did. So, when feeling lonely, turn to the One Who has *"borne our griefs, and carried our sorrows"* (Isaiah 53:4). Since He has known true loneliness, He can help you.

Too often we are tempted to dwell on our losses and bereavements. Another valuable lesson to learn is that of thankfulness. In the midst of suffering, Paul learned to rejoice in the Lord, regardless of his circumstances. He said, *"In every thing give thanks: for this is the will of God in Christ Jesus concerning you"* (1 Thessalonians 5:18). We can be thankful that we have God's presence, promises, protection, and provision. Further, we can be grateful for the time He gave us to enjoy those people or blessings that we have lost. Thank Him for the good times you had and the memories that you can continue to enjoy. Once you begin to thank the Lord, you will find yourself in His presence—*"Enter into his gates with thanksgiving, and into his courts with praise: be thankful unto him, and bless his name"* (Psalm 100:4).

If you are saved, you are never alone. If you have never received Jesus as your Savior, do so without delay. He is ready to cleanse your sin, calm your fear, and comfort your heart. Truly, *"God is our refuge and strength, a very present help in trouble"* (Psalm 46:1).

Never Alone

When in affliction's valley
I'm treading the road of care,
My Savior helps me to carry
My cross when heavy to bear,
Though all around me is darkness,
Earthly joys all flown;
My Savior whispers His promise,
"I never will leave thee alone."

No, never alone, No, never alone;
He promised never to leave me,
Never to leave me alone.

(Author Unknown – Third Verse and Chorus of the Hymn, *Never Alone*)

Day Eighteen

Wait On the Lord

"Wait on the LORD: be of good courage, and he shall strengthen thine heart: wait, I say, on the LORD"
—Psalm 27:14.

Most of us do not like to wait for anything. We have grown accustomed to getting what we want when we want it. We have access to fast food, overnight delivery, and instant messaging. Though modern conveniences have made it easier to satisfy our material longings, nothing invented by man will make God move any faster.

Waiting usually involves inconvenience and can cause great frustration. If you easily become irritated when stuck in traffic or waiting in a line, you probably struggle when God delays in answering your prayers. Impatience is a natural weakness found in our flesh, and patience is a virtue. Perhaps you are facing a trial which has been a challenge to endure. What can you do? *"Wait on the LORD."* Let's consider God's remedy for impatient souls.

A Command

In many areas of life we have choices. For instance, when ordering something online, we can choose how we want to receive it. If we are not in a hurry, we select standard shipping, but if we want it quickly, we choose expedited shipping. It would be nice if we had similar options when it comes to receiving answers to prayer, but we don't. God simply commands, *"Wait on the LORD."* He may move quickly, or He may delay. Like the psalmist, we can pray, *"make haste unto me, O God: thou art my help and my deliverer; O LORD, make no tarrying"* (Psalm 70:5). However, we have no right to complain when He is slow to deliver us. Neither should we become discouraged when He delays in answering our requests. When the Lord works at what seems to be a sluggish pace, we must remember that He knows best. God, in His wisdom, has made it clear that there are times in which we must wait.

It is impossible to wait on the Lord without the right attitude. The word *wait* implies not only the action of resting but also the attitude of expecting. It involves faith, knowing that God is in control of our situation. When a pressing need arises, talk to the Lord about it. Pray something like, "Lord, this is a big problem, and I would like an answer soon. Since your timing is perfect, I will wait for You to help when You know is best."

At times, we are tempted to rush ahead of God. Instead of trusting Him, we become anxious and act unwisely. This was the case with Saul. The Philistines had gathered to fight against Israel, and Saul was instructed to wait for Samuel the prophet to show him how to proceed. When things looked desperate, Saul panicked and took matters into his own hands. Instead of waiting for the prophet to make a sacrifice to the Lord, Saul did it himself. As a result, *"Samuel said to Saul, Thou*

> Failing to wait on God can cost you dearly.

hast done foolishly: thou hast not kept the commandment of the LORD thy God...now thy kingdom shall not continue" (1 Samuel 13:13). By failing to wait, Saul lost his kingdom. When we refuse to wait on the Lord, it can cost us dearly too.

Knowing our tendency to be impatient, the Lord repeated the command to wait in our text. Not only does the verse begin by saying, *"Wait on the LORD,"* it also ends with the same command, *"wait, I say, on the LORD."* Since it is mentioned twice, we should be twice as careful to obey it!

Courage

After being instructed to wait, God told us how to do it—*"be of good courage."* Webster defines *courage* as "Bravery...that quality of mind which enables men to encounter danger and difficulties with firmness, or without fear or depression of spirits."[5] Courage is the opposite of fear. Fear worries about what will happen while we are waiting upon God. Courage maintains hope that the Lord will deliver us, allowing us to maintain a cheerful disposition while we wait for Him to work.

Why would God tell us to be brave and courageous while waiting on Him? Because it is not easy to wait! It is easier to become discouraged. In fact, discouragement is a lack of courage. So, the way to avoid discouragement is to be courageous. Just as exercising courage is a choice, so is being discouraged. By saying, *"be of good courage,"* the Lord counsels us to make the right choice. It's like He

---

[5] Noah Webster, *Noah Webster's 1828 Dictionary of American English* (Franklin: e-Sword, 2000-2014), Digital Library.

said, "I want you to wait for me, but don't get discouraged in the process. Maintain a good attitude and trust me."

You may ask, "But how do I not lose hope while waiting on God?" The psalmist gave us the solution. He said, *"I wait for the LORD, my soul doth wait, and in his word do I hope"* (Psalm 130:5). We maintain hope by looking in God's Word. So, when feeling down, spend some extra time reading the Bible. At times, it seems like our trials have no end in sight. We wonder how much longer we can hang on. We become tired and ready to give up. The man of God felt the same way, but his hope was restored. He said, *"My soul fainteth for thy salvation: but I hope in thy word"* (Psalm 119:81). The solution is simple. Wait upon God by meditating upon His Word. This will give you the courage to get through your extended seasons of disappointment.

> A waiting heart is a hopeful heart.

Consolation

While waiting, we must fight off the temptation to think that the Lord has forgotten us or failed us. By maintaining hope, we secure a great blessing—*"he shall strengthen thine heart."* Along with the command to wait, God has promised the ability to do so. Is your heart faint? He will strengthen it!

When our physical heart is weak, the whole body suffers. In like manner, when the inner man is faint, we are affected mentally, emotionally, and spiritually. A strong heart, therefore, will make us fit to remain faithful to the Lord. What a promise—*"he shall strengthen thine heart"*!

Notice Who does the strengthening—God does. That makes it supernatural. We will be strong enough to endure any trial, no matter how long it lasts. Since God never runs out of strength, we can count on a steady supply of it. Our hearts can be happy and healthy regardless of how long we must wait. If waiting provides God's strength, we must conclude that it is well worth the wait.

Conclusion

Though we are not naturally inclined to wait, we must learn to do so when it comes to spiritual matters. If you have grown weary in waiting, have courage. God has a plan for all of His delays and provides hope through His Word. If you look with expectation for God's help, He will strengthen your heart and provide great victory. He has promised, *"they that wait upon the* LORD *shall renew their strength; they shall mount up with wings as eagles; they shall run, and not be weary; and they shall walk, and not faint"* (Isaiah 40:31). As God has helped you in the past, He will do it yet again. Wait on Him!

"O send out thy light and thy truth: let them lead me; let them bring me unto thy holy hill, and to thy tabernacles" —Psalm 43:3.

Day Nineteen

Light My Candle

"For thou wilt light my candle: the LORD my God will enlighten my darkness" —Psalm 18:28.

We may wish that every day could be bright and sunny, but that is not how life works. As surely as there is light, there is also darkness. Gloomy clouds roll in through disturbing circumstances, causing fear and fretting. As believers, *"we know that all things work together for good to them that love God, to them who are the called according to his purpose"* (Romans 8:28). The Lord will only allow trying times to afflict us to work for His glory and our benefit. Though we may experience great disappointments, God has promised that He will not leave us in darkness. Let's consider our text in more detail and see how it applies to our lives.

Our Cry

Consider the cry of David's heart. Instead of running to earthly comforters, he spoke directly to God about his plight. He cried out, *"thou wilt light my candle."* No human agent has power to dispel the darkness that looms in the soul. You cannot entertain it away, worry it away, or medicate it away. Spiritual battles must be fought with spiritual weaponry. Why not run to *"the Light of the world"* to brighten your outlook? If you do, you will be able to testify like David, *"I waited patiently for the LORD; and he inclined unto me, and heard my cry"* (Psalm 40:1).

Our Confidence

You may say, "I have prayed, but nothing has happened." If that is the case, your honesty betrays your lack of faith. Certainly, we must *"doubt not"* if we hope to secure a blessing from God (Matthew 21:21). Notice the confidence that David had—*"thou wilt light my candle."* He was fully persuaded that God would send the necessary light. Life was no picnic for David as he fled for his life from Saul. His days were dismal as his trial dragged on for months.

> Since God is Light, we know He give us light.

Despite the extended affliction, he never lost hope that God would send light. Oh, be confident that your Father loves you and will set your candle aflame as soon as He knows it is best!

Our Calm

Our text verse also speaks of calm—*"thou wilt light my candle."* Light dispels darkness and the anxiety associated with it. Once your candle is lit and you can see your situation clearly, peace will flood your soul. Too many of God's children borrow trouble when they should beg for light. As a lit candle quiets the hearts of little children during a power outage, so God seeks to settle the hearts of His children during their trials. Expect a great calm to quell the storm clouds that hover about you.

Our Comfort

One more quality of candlelight is worth mentioning—comfort. The flame of God's light provides warmth to hearts that have grown cold, cheerfulness to the discouraged, and radiance for those in darkness. Praise God that His beams of love and mercy can outshine our doubts, fears, and troubles!

Conclusion

Don't allow your present trouble to unsettle you. Ask God to light your candle. Perhaps you have sat in darkness longer than necessary. Seek the Lord and wait patiently for Him. When faith is renewed, you can say with David, *"the LORD my God will enlighten my darkness."* Join in the chorus of the great hymn, "I sing through the shade and sunshine, I'll trust Him whatever befall; I sing for I cannot be silent – My Father planned it all."

"But though he cause grief, yet will he have compassion according to the multitude of his mercies" —Lamentations 3:32.

Day Twenty

Good from Grief

*"It is good for me that I have been afflicted;
that I might learn thy statutes"*
—Psalm 119:71.

If you are presently experiencing grief, you might be thinking, "What could possibly be good about grief?" That is an understandable reaction. I get it. I am tempted to think that way, at times, too. However, as Christians who seek to follow God and understand His ways, we are compelled to look past our own reasoning. Thankfully, truths like those contained in our text have been recorded to help us know God's ways more clearly.

The psalmist declared, *"It is good for me that I have been afflicted."* Noah Webster defined the word *affliction* as "the state of being afflicted; a state of pain, distress, or grief."[6] By definition, grief is often part of affliction. This is important because the testimony of the psalmist is that affliction (which includes grief) *"is good."* Okay, now that we have established that grief is good, we need to consider why it is so.

---

[6] Noah Webster, *Noah Webster's 1828 Dictionary of American English* (Franklin: e-Sword, 2000-2014), Digital Library.

Grief Teaches Us

The reason that grief and affliction are good for us is that we *"might learn."* The Hebrew word used for *learn* comes from a root word that means "to goad." A goad is a pointed device used to poke and prod an animal to move. The psalmist said the purpose of his affliction was that he would be goaded. He needed to be prodded to learn. Learn what? The *"statutes"* of God. Affliction and grief can be greatly used to get our attention focused more on the Lord.

Grief Corrects Us

Sometimes we need to be prodded because we are heading in the wrong direction. The psalmist admitted, *"Before I was afflicted I went astray: but now have I kept thy word"* (Psalm 119:67). His affliction was the result of straying from the Lord, but God used trouble to get him back on the right course. Isaiah said, *"All we like sheep have gone astray"* (Isaiah 53:6). Since we are prone to get off track, we need times of tribulation to redirect us.

When we become stubborn and refuse to move at all, we may need to be poked by affliction. Problems can be used to motivate us to get busy for the Lord to accomplish the work He has appointed us to do. When grief leads to renewed obedience it is good.

Grief Draws Us

Further, your experience with grief and affliction may not be a result of wrongdoing at all. It might simply be the instrument that God has designed to prod you to seek Him more earnestly. When trouble enters our lives, we tend to seek Him more than when all is going well. Perhaps the Lord is using your problems to draw you closer to Himself and enrich your life with His grace. If so, that is God using your grief to bring about good.

Grief Equips Us

Finally, grief can be used to prepare us for greater usefulness. Webster aptly said, "Some virtues are seen only in affliction."[7] When Paul suffered the loss of his health, the Lord told him why, saying, *"My grace is sufficient for thee: for my strength is made perfect in weakness"* (2 Corinthians 12:9). Paul's loss led to God's enablement! Consider a great illustration of this. Five days after my mother's funeral, my dad fell and was taken to the hospital. On top of losing his wife, he was in considerable pain and discomfort. Through the years, he has learned to give thanks in all things. Wasting no time, within a few hours at the hospital he witnessed to one of the nurses who attended to him. As a result, that nurse received the Lord as her Savior. After several days, my father was moved to a nursing home for rehabilitation. One of the staff ladies went to his room to complete the admission paperwork. She, too, heard the gospel and got saved. After she prayed to receive Christ, she thanked my father and showed great excitement when he promised to give her some discipleship material. A few days later, while outside getting some fresh air, my dad met a man who had just arrived to visit his mother. Dad struck up a conversation with him and gave

---

[7] Noah Webster, *Noah Webster's 1828 Dictionary of American English* (Franklin: e-Sword, 2000-2014), Digital Library.

him a tract. After the man finished visiting his mother, he stopped and spoke to my father again. The man had a heavy heart, and the Lord used my dad to present the gospel to him. Soon, he was kneeling on the sidewalk in front of the nursing home, praying to receive Jesus as His Savior. The next day, a lady from the Physical Therapy department went to my father's room to go over his discharge papers. You can guess what happened. She too was gloriously saved. She was so happy that she gave my dad a big hug! As you can imagine, my father was filled with joy that God had used him to reach others.

Was my dad grieving the loss of his wife? Yes. Did he experience pain and affliction from his fall? Certainly, however, he understood that grief can lead to great good. Instead of sitting around feeling sorry for himself, he learned to see that his afflictions created great opportunities to serve the Lord. How do you handle grief? Will you allow God's pokes and prods to motivate you to greater service?

Conclusion

Believe it or not, our grief can actually be a source of comfort. Did not David say to the Lord, *"thy rod and thy staff they comfort me"* (Psalm 23:4)? The Good Shepherd makes great use of the rod and staff to redirect our steps, draw us closer to Himself, and use us in greater ways. How comforting to know that God can use our grief and affliction for good! May we learn to say, *"It is good for me that I have been afflicted."*

Day Twenty One

Battling Bitterness

"Looking diligently lest any man fail of the grace of God; lest any root of bitterness springing up trouble you, and thereby many be defiled" —Hebrews 12:15.

Every time that person's name is mentioned or that traumatic event comes to your mind, bitter feelings well up in your heart. You know it is wrong, but it keeps coming back. What can you do?

In our garden, weeds with very sharp thorns sprung up. Pulling the weeds was no easy task because, not only were the roots deep, they also had tiny sharp thorns. So, even pulling the weeds by the roots was a painful process. It was no easy task to dig down and get the whole weed out of the ground, but failure to do so meant that we would continue to deal with the problem. Is this not a picture of dealing with bitterness? Bitterness is a root. Scripture calls it *"the root of bitterness."* Unless bitterness is pulled out, it will continue to come back. Like working with a thorny weed, dealing with the root can be a painful experience. However, failure to address your bitterness can lead to more problems down the road. So, let's learn some lessons to better equip us to fight bitterness.

Bitterness Springs Up

As we mentioned, bitterness is like a weed that springs up. You know you are bitter when you allow an injustice (or perceived injustice) to fester in your heart. You bring it up and think about it from time to time. Sometimes, you can hardly get it out of your mind. You are like a lawyer who is on the lookout for evidence to build a case against your offender. Does this describe you at times? When you find yourself rehearsing the wrongs done to you, stop and realize that you have a *"root of bitterness springing up."* Once that root shoots up, it will begin to inflict pain.

Bitterness Troubles You

The first victim of bitterness is you! By choosing to be bitter, you hurt yourself. Bitterness causes self-inflicted injuries. If you fail to deal with it, it will *"trouble you."* While we may convince ourselves that bitterness will bring pain to others, it first and foremost injures us. We have to remember that the *"heart is deceitful above all things, and desperately wicked"* (Jeremiah 17:9). Our corrupt hearts lie to us and convince us that there is some satisfaction in getting angry and harboring bitterness toward someone. The more you dwell on the problem, the more miserable you become. How happy does that angry disposition make you feel? One of the words used to define *bitter* is *wormwood.* Wormwood is a plant that produces a nauseous taste. If you want to feel sick to your stomach, continue to harbor bitterness in your heart.

Bitterness Defiles Many

Though the first casualty of bitterness is the one who has it in his or her heart, it will soon affect others. In the end, many will *"be defiled."* This happens in two ways.

First, people will be defiled through gossip. Bitter people find it difficult to keep their feelings to themselves. An old saying comes to mind—*misery loves company.* The word *defiled* refers to being contaminated. A bad attitude spreads to others like the flu. Through critical comments and a sour spirit, the bitter person infects all who will listen. Typically, bitter people vent their frustrations to those they are close to such as friends, spouses, or workmates. Sadly, bitterness is often passed from parents to their children.

> Bitterness leads to retaliation.

Are you guilty of contaminating the people you care about with your bitter attitude? Is that what you really want to do? Even worse than injuring others is to hurt God. Included on the list of seven abominations is, *"...he that soweth discord among brethren"* (Proverbs 6:19). God hates it when we allow bitterness to lead to pitting one believer against another.

Second, people will be defiled through acts of vengeance. Bitterness may lead to lashing out against the person who has offended you. The more you consider the injustices that you have suffered, the easier it becomes to justify getting even. You may suppress those feelings for a while, but sooner or later, that case you have been building is going to come out in an ugly tirade. Bitterness is like a volcano, capable of erupting without any warning. Not only will the one receiving your tongue lashing be defiled, but so will everyone else who hears it. Is this what you want to happen in your home, at church, or in the office? Oh, how terrible bitterness can be! When tempted to seek revenge, remember the exhortation spoken by Paul, *"Dearly beloved, avenge not yourselves, but rather give place unto wrath: for it is written, Vengeance is mine; I will repay, saith the Lord"* (Romans 12:19). When God judges someone, He never makes a mistake. However, when we retaliate in anger, we sin—*"For the wrath of man worketh not the righteousness of God"* (James 1:20).

Bitterness Must Be Guarded Against

We are exhorted, to be *"looking diligently"* at our spiritual condition. It takes work and constant oversight to prevent bitterness. Thankfully, we are given some tips on preventing bitterness from taking root. *"Follow peace with all men, and holiness, without which no man shall see the Lord"* (Hebrews 12:14). If we pursue a peaceful relationship with *"all men"* and allow *"holiness"* to guide our actions, we will prevent the seeds of bitterness from settling in our hearts. Let's consider both ideas.

First, we are to pursue peace. Whether we want to or not, we must act peaceably towards everybody, including those who have hurt us. Jesus said, *"Blessed are the peacemakers: for they shall be called the children of God"* (Matthew 5:9). *Blessed* means "happy." Bitter people are miserable, but peacemakers are happy. If you want to change your disposition, seek peace.

That happens, first of all, by forgiving your offender. Bitterness usually stems from failing to forgive another. The word *forgive* has the idea of treating your offender as not guilty. It involves sending away the offense. If we truly forgive someone, there is nothing to bring up and become bitter about. If you want to have peace, it starts in your own heart. Jesus taught that forgiveness must be sincere—*"from your hearts forgive"* (Matthew 18:35). Get rid of the offense. Get it out of your heart. This is done through prayer. Jesus said, *"And when ye stand praying, forgive, if ye have ought against any"* (Mark 11:25). Confess that you have bitterness in your heart. Then, tell the Lord that you forgive that person and want the bitterness gone. That is a prayer He is ready to answer!

We seek peace, secondly, by guarding our interactions with our foes. That means, when they do something to provoke us, we do not respond in the same manner. Peter reminds us, *"For this is thankworthy, if a man for conscience toward God endure grief, suffering wrongfully...For even hereunto were ye called"* (1 Peter 2:19, 21). Being a peacemaker means that we swallow our pride and refrain from retaliating. Whether we like it or not, we are *"called"* to suffer wrongfully. That may go against the grain of our carnal nature, but we must allow the Holy Spirit to control us, not the flesh.

Finally, we can promote peace by showing kindness to our enemies. *"Bless them which persecute you: bless, and curse not...Therefore if thine enemy hunger, feed him; if he thirst, give him drink"* (Romans 12:14, 20). This principle is summed up this way, *"Be not overcome of evil, but overcome evil with good"* (Romans 12:21). When you purposely act in a kind, Christ-like manner, you will

> We can overcome evil with good.

overcome the evil that wants to control your heart. Being a peacemaker does not always mean that you will successfully get others to treat you well, but it does mean that you have made peace in your heart and extended peace to the other party.

Second, we are to allow holiness to rule our conduct. God commands, *"Follow peace with all men, and holiness."* Instead of allowing your flesh to dictate your actions, yield to the Holy Spirit. Our responses to ill treatment must be holy, not fleshly. We are exhorted, *"Walk in the Spirit, and ye shall not fulfil the lust of the flesh"* (Galatians 5:16). Allow His promptings and conviction to govern your conduct.

Bitterness will try to take root, but we can prevent it by diligently guarding our hearts, seeking peace with others, forgiving our offenders, and responding to mistreatment in a holy manner. As we discussed earlier, dealing with bitterness may be painful, but it will prevent a lot of problems for everybody.

Bitterness Can Lead to Other Sins

If we fail to deal with bitterness, more evil will follow. After warning us about bitterness, the writer of Hebrews tells us why we should guard against it. He said, *"Lest there be any fornicator, or profane person, as Esau, who for one morsel of meat sold his birthright"* (Hebrews 12:16). As we know, Esau was a fleshly man. After he sold his birthright, the seeds of bitterness began to take root. Then, when Jacob stole Esau's blessing, the bitterness came out. Esau hated his brother and developed a plan that he would carry out once his father had died. He said, *"...then will I slay my brother Jacob"* (Genesis 27:41). Like Esau's bitterness led to wicked intentions, so can yours. If you allow bitterness to boil in your heart, it will be dangerous when it spills out.

Conclusion

We will all experience injustices. They can be painful and life-altering. However, we must not allow bitterness to take root in our hearts. If we do, it will create more trouble in our souls. Then, our bitterness will defile many others, even people we love. If we are not careful, bitterness will lead to either physical or verbal retaliation. By God's grace, we can have victory over bitterness by forgiving our offenders, guarding our interactions with them, and being kind to them. The Holy Spirit will enable us to set aside the desires of our flesh if we yield to Him. It starts with wanting to put away bitterness. Are you ready to take the necessary steps to guard your heart and home from this terrible sin? All who do will experience brighter days ahead. May the Lord grant you His grace to battle bitterness!

"Let all bitterness, and wrath, and anger, and clamour, and evil speaking, be put away from you, with all malice" (Ephesians 4:31).

"Thou rulest the raging of the sea: when the waves thereof arise, thou stillest them"

-Psalm 89:9.

Day Twenty Two

Waves of Affliction

"The LORD on high is mightier than the noise of many waters, yea, than the mighty waves of the sea"
—Psalm 93:4.

Water is an amazing part of God's creation. It has power to sustain life and the ability to take it away. Great harm can be caused by having either too little or too much water. In the Bible, the words *waves* and *floods* often refer to threatening trials. Waves of affliction toss us around and carry us far from the peaceful shores we desire. At times, the floods of trouble are so severe that it becomes difficult to keep our noses above water. Let's consider what we can learn from our waves of affliction.

Describing the Waves

Waves are powerful. Waves can be strong enough to break mighty ships in pieces as Paul experienced. They can also render navigation systems useless as the disciples discovered while in a raging storm on the Sea of Galilee. Previously, while on smooth waters, the disciples controlled the direction of their ship, but everything changed once the wind began to blow. *"But the ship was now in the midst of the sea, tossed with waves: for the wind was contrary"*

(Matthew 14:24). Their vessel was *"tossed"* by powerful waves. Trials can have a similar influence on us and, if not handled properly, can knock our lives off course. As *"the wind was contrary"* to the disciples, it will be against you too. When a big wave crashes upon you, it will be easy to lose your footing and stumble. Therefore, we must maintain a healthy respect for waves of affliction.

Waves are persistent. If you visit the coast, you will observe how the waves come ashore one after another. They never seem to stop. Life is much the same way. One wave of trouble often comes after another. This was the experience of the psalmist. He said, *"The floods have lifted up, O LORD, the floods have lifted up their voice; the floods lift up their waves"* (Psalm 93:3). Notice that the words *floods* and *waves* are in the plural form. He was not threatened by one wave or a single flood; he faced many of them! Life is going to give us multiple problems. When you feel like nobody else has it as bad as you do, think again. Peter reminds us that *"the same afflictions are accomplished in your brethren that are in the world"* (1 Peter 5:9). Many other Christians have *"the same afflictions."* So, don't feel sorry for yourself. Instead of being overwhelmed by your problems, learn how to deal with them.

Waves are perilous. Sailors know the danger that waves pose to both man and ship. Many mariners have been swept off the deck into the raging waters never to be seen again. Sadly, some believers allow afflictions to carry them out to seas of worldliness. Rather than cling to God, they return to sinful vices to help them cope with their problems. Straying from God in a storm is not safe. The only way we will survive is to turn to the Lord. The disciples faced a threatening storm—*"And there arose a great storm of wind, and the waves beat into the ship, so that it was now full"* (Mark 4:37). How did they survive? They went to Jesus for help. Notice what the Savior did—*"he arose, and rebuked the wind, and said unto the sea, Peace, be still. And the wind ceased, and there was a great calm"* (Mark 4:39). As He calmed the threatening waves for them, He can do the same for you! Seeking Him is the best way to handle your troubles.

> It's not safe to stray from God in a storm.

Waves can be punitive. While some of our trials are meant to test us, others are meant to correct us. At times, the Lord will send waves of trouble into the life of a backslider to get him to consider his ways. When Jonah disobeyed God, he was cast into the sea and swallowed by the whale. He had time to contemplate the error of his ways and repented. In his prayer, he said, *"For thou hadst cast me into the deep, in the midst of the seas; and the floods compassed me about: all thy billows and thy waves passed over me"* (Jonah 2:3). God had used *"the deep...the seas...the floods...billows...waves"* to get his attention. Notice, in particular, that Jonah mentioned, *"thy waves."* He knew that they were God's waves sent to discipline him. When we stray from God, we can expect wave after wave of affliction to cause us to return to the Lord. The psalmist also understood God's use of waves to chasten. He prayed, *"Thy wrath lieth hard upon me, and thou hast afflicted me with all thy waves"* (Psalm 88:7). Many troubles can be avoided simply by living right!

Dealing with the Waves

Now that we have described how waves can affect us, let us turn our attention to how we should deal with them. Because our strength is small, we need to turn to the Master of the seas for help. He has the power to calm our hearts during the storms of life. Here are some steps we can take.

Talk to the Lord about your troubles. When the waves threatened the psalmist, he told God about his struggles—*"The floods have lifted up, O LORD, the floods have lifted up their voice; the floods lift up their waves"* (Psalm 93:3). Does the Lord already know about your problems? Yes. So, why tell Him what He already knows?

> Prayer expresses dependence upon God.

We pray to express our dependence upon Him. A scenario in my marriage illustrates this well. Many times, while living in Africa, we had poisonous snakes enter our yard. When my wife saw one, she did not say, "Dave, please come and take care of this snake." She simply yelled, "Dave, snake!" She made me aware of the problem, knowing that I would run to her aid. It works the same way with God. When our hearts are overwhelmed, all we need to do is cry out in faith, *"the floods lift up their waves,"* and He will step in to handle them.

Realize that God is bigger than your troubles. After the psalmist made God aware of his problem, he revealed why He called upon Him with such confidence. He said, *"The LORD on high is mightier than the noise of many waters, yea, than the mighty waves of the sea"* (Psalm 93:4). He knew that God was *"mightier"* than anything he would face. We would do well to believe the song that we teach little children—*My God is so big, so strong and so mighty. There's nothing my God cannot do*! Whatever your problem might be, God is *"mightier."*

Remember God's presence amidst your troubles. In Isaiah's day, God promised His people, *"When thou passest through the waters, I will be with thee; and through the rivers, they shall not overflow thee"* (Isaiah 43:2). What reassuring words! Though the waves will come, they will not destroy us. The Creator of the waters said, *"I will be with thee."* What more do I need? If the Lord is with me, I am safe, sheltered, and secure. Consider Peter. Despite the violent waves about him, he was able to walk on water because he was with Jesus. When the winds begin to howl and the waves start to mount, you can find shelter with the Rock of your salvation.

Look at your troubles as opportunities. When people visit the ocean, the presence of waves can bring two different reactions. Large waves keep the average beachgoer out of the water, but big waves draw the avid surfer into the water. One dreads the waves and the other delights in them. Like surfers see waves as opportunities, we should too. Consider Peter once again. The powerful wind and waves gave him a great opportunity to see God work miraculously. After all, he was able to walk on water! As the storm allowed Peter to exercise his faith in the Lord, we can express our confidence in God when waves of affliction threaten us. If we trust Him, God will show Himself mighty on our behalf.

Keep your eyes on God, not on your troubles. Although Peter did walk on water, he also almost drowned because he took his eyes off Jesus. Fortunately, he realized his error and quickly refocused on the Lord—*"But when he saw the wind boisterous, he was afraid; and beginning to sink, he cried, saying, Lord, save me"* (Matthew 14:30). Like Peter, we may handle our storms well initially, but then get distracted by the waves of affliction that surround us. When that happens, fear sets in and our faltering faith endangers our condition. As soon as we take our eyes off the Lord, our souls begin to sink in despair. If you have begun to sink in sorrow, cry out, *"Lord, save me."* As Jesus *"stretched forth his hand, and caught"* Peter, He wants to do the same for you (Matthew 14:31).

Waves of affliction will threaten us all. Let's determine to focus on the Lord, not on our problems. Those who trust God will be able to testify with the psalmist, *"Thou rulest the raging of the sea: when the waves thereof arise, thou stillest them"* (Psalm 89:9).

Day Twenty Three

Promised Rest

"I will give you rest" —Matthew 11:28.

Troubles tend to wear us out. A heavy burden carried for a long time makes one weary. What is needed is rest, and that is just what our Lord promises to give His children. Jesus said, *"Come unto me, all ye that labour and are heavy laden, and I will give you rest"* (Matthew 11:28). The rest He promised is for the inner man—*"ye shall find rest unto your souls"* (11:29).

When transporting a heavy object, we find that we can carry it farther if we take a short break and rest. Rest renews our strength and enables us to keep pressing on. As rest is important to the body, it is also vital to the soul. Too many of God's children have needlessly been crushed by the weight of life's trials. Instead of seeking God's rest, they have labored to carry burdens that God never intended for them to carry alone.

The first step in finding rest for the soul is to turn to Jesus. He invites all who are troubled, saying, *"Come unto me."* Go to Jesus and allow Him to carry your heartaches. He pleads with us, *"Take my yoke upon you, and learn of me; for I am meek and lowly in heart: and ye shall find rest unto your souls"* (11:29). In Christ's day, the yoke was a wooden instrument often used to join two oxen for the purpose of pulling a plow or a cart. The yoke enabled the oxen to work together as a team and ensured that one animal would not be called upon to carry the entire load. When we accept Christ's yoke, He gives us rest because He carries the weight.

David understood this principle well. He said, *"Cast thy burden upon the LORD, and he shall sustain thee: he shall never suffer the righteous to be moved"* (Psalm 55:22). God wants to carry your burden for you. If you cast your troubles upon Him, you will find great relief. Further, you will never *"be moved."* The word *moved* refers to slipping and falling. Carrying heavy burdens can make us weak-kneed and prone to fall. However, when we allow the Lord to carry our sorrows, the crushing weight which once caused us to stumble disappears. Our hearts will be lightened, and a bounce to our step will be restored. Praise God!

Are you presently experiencing a heavy heart? Are you struggling to carry a difficult burden? It is not God's plan for you to bear your burdens alone. Jesus invites you, *"Come unto me."* We are promised rest only when we cast our burden upon Him. Without obtaining the rest He offers, we will eventually faint and bring dishonor to our Savior. Stop trying to carry your burdens in your own strength. Allow Jesus to lift your load.

> Stop carrying the burdens that God wants to carry for you.

We must never forget that the Lord loves us dearly. The apostle Peter reminds us of God's concern for each of His children. He said, *"Casting all your care upon him; for he careth for you"* (1 Peter 5:7). He cares for you too much to expect you to bear any burden by yourself. That is why you are instructed to cast *"all your care upon him."*

Do not look on your present burden as a curse. It might be meant to draw you closer to the Lord and allow you to experience His divine assistance. If so, your burden is actually a blessing!

"But what things were gain to me, those I counted loss for Christ"
-Philippians 3:7.

Day Twenty Four

Painful Loss

"Son of man, behold, I take away from thee the desire of thine eyes with a stroke: yet neither shalt thou mourn nor weep" —Ezekiel 24:16.

Many believers serve God only when it is convenient. This was not the case with Ezekiel. The Lord told him that He would suddenly *"take away"* the desire of his eyes, referring to the wife he loved so dearly. To make things more difficult, the prophet was to refrain from all outward expressions of grief as a sign to the people who were in captivity. As Ezekiel did not mourn publicly for the loss of his wife, neither would the Jews living in Chaldea display their grief when Jerusalem would fall. That was the picture that God wanted to portray through Ezekiel's reaction. Now that we have considered the event, let us make some applications.

Remain Faithful

Despite overwhelming grief, we can remain faithful to God. Ezekiel testified, *"So I spake unto the people in the morning: and at even my wife died; and I did in the morning as I was commanded"* (24:18). He did not allow his loss to hinder his service but did as he was told to do.

Do you allow problems to hinder you from serving God? It is typical for us to seek comfort when our hearts are heavy. Rather than ministering to the needs of others we hope someone will minister to us. Maintaining such an attitude may lead to putting too much focus on ourselves. In most cases, despite our troubles, we still have others who depend upon us to help them. Ezekiel provides a great example to follow, putting God's interests ahead of his own.

Control Emotions

Emotions can be controlled. God told the prophet not to *"mourn nor weep."* This is not a command to every believer. It was unique to Ezekiel. However, this account does teach us an important lesson. Even in difficult times, it is possible to keep our grief in check. While we are not forbidden to shed tears when we lose a loved one, we are instructed not to be consumed with uncontrollable grief. Paul put it this way, *"that ye sorrow not, even as others which have no hope"* (1 Thessalonians 4:13). Because Christians do have hope, we should grieve differently than unbelievers. Sadness is natural, but our reaction must not be out of control. Like Ezekiel, we can guard our hearts from unruly emotional outbursts. While I am glad that I am permitted to cry when overwhelming grief strikes, I am also happy that I do not have to wallow in unhealthy despair.

> Even in sorrow, we have hope!

Allow Loss to Be Used for God's Glory

What is dearest to us may be taken and used for God's glory. Ezekiel's wife died suddenly. There is no indication that she was in failing health or that she was being judged for a sinful life. In fact, since Ezekiel delighted in her so much, she must have been a godly lady. Their relationship was undoubtedly good and proper, but despite their love for each other, the prophet's wife was taken from the man of God. We must remember that serving the Lord does not exempt us from hardships or heartaches. Don't hang on too tightly to *"the desire of thine eyes."* Never allow any earthly desire to come before the Lord. Some people wrongly give up on God when they lose someone or something precious to them. Asaph declared that his chief desire was the Lord, saying, *"Whom have I in heaven but thee? and there is none upon earth that I desire beside thee"* (Psalm 73:25). When God is our greatest desire, we will loosen our grip on all other desires, even good ones. Loss can be extremely painful, but one thing we will never lose is the presence of God. The Lord said, *"I will never leave thee, nor forsake thee"* (Hebrews 13:5). When the dearest to your heart is taken from you, remember that the *"eternal God is thy refuge, and underneath are the everlasting arms"* (Deuteronomy 33:27). He will sustain you.

> No believer is exempt from heartache.

Conclusion

God had a plan for Ezekiel's loss, and He has one for yours too. Though you may not see it quite yet, in due time it will be revealed. Trust Him and do not be *"swallowed up with overmuch sorrow"* (2 Corinthians 2:7).

"The fear of man bringeth a snare: but whoso putteth his trust in the LORD shall be safe"
-Proverbs 29:25.

Day Twenty Five

The Spirit of Fear

"For God hath not given us the spirit of fear; but of power, and of love, and of a sound mind" —2 Timothy 1:7.

Fear can be good or bad. Fear is good when it prevents us from doing bad things, but fear is bad when it prevents us from doing good things. Some fear is healthy to have because it helps us to avoid trouble. Fear makes us careful when walking across a busy street. It helps us to follow the laws of the land. Most importantly, fear motivates us to submit to God and abstain from sin. This is what Solomon meant when he said, *"The fear of the LORD is to hate evil"* (Proverbs 8:13).

What is mentioned in our text, however, refers to an unhealthy kind of fear. The word *fear* implies timidity, which can indicate weakness and a lack of courage. In context, Paul warned Timothy not to allow fear to hinder his service for God. Perhaps you have experienced this bad kind of fear. It was in your heart to do something for God, but the *"spirit of fear"* came upon you and prevented you from following through. Unfortunately, the *"spirit of fear"* not only gets the best of some people, it also enslaves them. Such people live in defeat and never reach their potential for the Lord. Do you battle the *"spirit of fear"*? If so, there is hope.

How Does Fear Affect Us?

The apostle John said, *"...fear hath torment"* (1 John 4:18). It produces anxiety. It cripples us from doing what is right. It weakens the inner man. It imagines things that may never happen. Fear robs us of the peace of God. It hinders our usefulness. It causes us to be suspicious. It produces cowardice. It demoralizes. It brings regrets. It focuses on circumstances, not on God. Fear affects us emotionally, physically, mentally, and spiritually. What a horrible thing fear can be! If fear has affected you in any of these ways, determine to face it and overcome it.

One of the biggest detriments of fear is that it holds people captive. Though fear may be a spirit, it does not proceed from the Holy Spirit. God's Spirit brings liberty and peace—*"where the Spirit of the Lord is, there is liberty"* (2 Corinthians 3:17). When we allow fear to hinder us from doing what is right, we find ourselves in bondage and laden with guilt. It is helpful to realize that bondage and fear feed off each other, creating a vicious cycle of torment and entrapment. Paul wrote to the brethren in Rome, saying, *"For ye have not received the spirit of bondage again to fear"* (Romans 8:15). It has never been God's plan for His people to be brought into bondage and fear. If you suffer from the *"spirit of fear,"* you must determine to stop the cycle. We will discuss this more later, but you must start by refusing to allow fear to hinder you from doing what is right. Once

> Fear brings bondage.

you yield to fear, it becomes your master. That is what Paul referred to when he said, *"Know ye not, that to whom ye yield yourselves servants to obey, his servants ye are to whom ye obey...?"* (Romans 6:16).

Where Does Fear Come From?

Identifying the source of our fears is the first step to victory. Our text reminds us that fear does not come from God. In fact, He gives the opposite, which is the spirit *"of power, and of love, and of a sound mind."* So, where does fear come from? It stems from external and internal influences.

The Christian has many foes in this world. The devil and his demons have opposed God's people throughout history. When trying to help the believers in Thessalonica, Paul testified, *"Satan hindered us"* (1 Thessalonians 2:18). Some people are more afraid of offending the devil than they are of disobeying God. Never fear Satan more than the Lord! We are also tempted to fear ungodly people who try to intimidate us and silence our testimony for the Lord. If you fear what others might do or say, you have the wrong kind of fear. We should not fear the devil or man. John reminds us, *"Ye are of God, little children, and have overcome them: because greater is he that is in you, than he that is in the world"* (1 John 4:4).

We also face inner fears. Our hearts and minds are not always as strong as we think. Even spiritual giants such as the apostle Paul faced emotional fear. He testified, *"...we were troubled on every side; without were fightings, within were fears"* (2 Corinthians 7:5). Fear comes from within our corrupt, unbelieving hearts. It is a weakness of our flesh. That is why the phrase, *"Fear not,"* is found dozens of times throughout the Bible. God knows that we are prone to fear. It should comfort us to understand that the Lord knows our frailties and has promised to strengthen us. Since many great men of faith were tempted to fear, we know that we will be tempted also. The key is to understand where the fear comes from and face it Biblically.

What Can We Do About Fear?

Earlier, we mentioned an important step—do not yield to fear in the first place. Once you allow fear to grip your heart, you will be in bondage. Jesus said, *"Whosoever committeth sin is the servant of sin"* (John 8:34). Stop serving fear; it is a horrible master. Listen to your true Master Who says, *"Fear not."* It is a choice. Say to yourself, "Today, I am going to obey God, not fear." Victory starts by making the right choice.

If you are currently in bondage to fear, you need to be freed. Thankfully, the Word of God can set you free. *"And ye shall know the truth, and the truth shall make you free"* (John 8:32). Study your Bible and look up verses that can help you overcome fear. Today's reading provides several passages which you can study and meditate upon. Studying, however, is not enough. You must learn to recall the truths that you have learned and apply them when you are tempted to fear. Fight back using the Sword of the Lord, which is the Bible!

Finally, the most important thing you can do is trust God. Faith is the heart of the matter. Faith brings victory, and fear brings defeat. David was a mighty man of valor. He was the only person in Israel courageous enough to face

Goliath. However, even he faced fear. Notice his solution when fear tried to get the best of him. He prayed, *"What time I am afraid, I will trust in thee. In God I will praise his word, in God I have put my trust; I will not fear what flesh can do unto me."* (Psalm 56:3-4). David rehearsed God's Word, prayed, relied upon God, and realized that man was no match for him with God on his side. If you follow the same plan that David did, you will have the same results. Faith is the victory!

"For thou, O God, hast proved us: thou hast tried us, as silver is tried" -Psalm 66:10.

Day Twenty Six

The Furnace of Affliction

"Behold, I have refined thee, but not with silver; I have chosen thee in the furnace of affliction" —Isaiah 48:10.

Two words in the above passage tend to make us feel uncomfortable: *furnace* and *affliction*. A furnace is a place of fire and extreme heat, and affliction refers to pain, distress, and grief. We would not naturally choose to enter a furnace of affliction, but it is exactly where many great Christians have found themselves. Thankfully, our text also has two encouraging words: *refined* and *chosen*. The fires of affliction are what refine us and equip us to be chosen for God's service. Let's consider how God uses the furnace of affliction in our lives.

A Personal Furnace

We find two more words in the above verse that have meaning for us: *I* and *thee*. The *I* refers to God. We are assured that He sees us in our time of suffering. David realized this, saying, *"For he hath not despised nor abhorred the affliction of the afflicted; neither hath he hid his face from him; but when he cried unto him, he heard"* (Psalm 22:24). How wonderful to know that God knows all about our trouble and hears us when we cry unto Him! If

He has us in His furnace, we also know that He is watching over us.

The second word, *thee*, shows that our afflictions are unique. What God has planned for you, He may not intend for another. Therefore, it is not wise to compare yourself with others who may not presently be experiencing difficulties. Always remember that the Lord deals with us as individuals and knows what is best for each of us. God's furnace is designed specifically to refine you, and He will not put you through more than you can bear.

A Painful Furnace

Pain is a part of life. It can be painful to get bad things out of our lives. For example, it hurts to have an inflamed appendix removed, but failure to do so can be fatal. Pain can also be necessary to enhance our lives. When we start an exercise program to improve our health, we know that we are going to experience some aches and pains. However, we are willing to suffer in order to be better in the end. As the old expression reminds us, "No pain, no gain."

As Christians, it can be painful to get sin out of our lives and righteousness into it. The furnace of affliction is used to do both. Most of us are not big fans of pain, but by definition, affliction includes pain. It would be nice if we could have "problem-free" problems, but it just doesn't work that way. At times, we are afflicted physically, mentally, or emotionally. Rather than crying out, "That's not fair!" we should seek to understand why we are in the furnace. Consider two common reasons.

First, afflictions can be the result of sin. This was the case with Israel. A few verses before Isaiah mentioned *"the furnace of affliction,"* he revealed why they had been put into it. Notice God's indictment upon Israel, *"I knew that thou art obstinate, and thy neck is an iron sinew, and thy brow brass"* (Isaiah 48:4). They were hardhearted, hardheaded, and stiff-necked. In other words, because of their stubbornness, God chose a series of fiery trials to purify them. When we become reluctant to follow the Lord, we can expect painful problems too. Like God has not given up on Israel, He will not give up on us either.

Second, afflictions are used in our sanctification. While it is good for us to examine our lives for sin when afflictions come, we should realize that troubles are not reserved exclusively for the backslider. Tribulation is common for the saint as well as the sinner. The truth is that good people are put in the furnace of affliction to make them even better. David said, *"Many are the afflictions of the righteous: but the LORD delivereth him out of them all"* (Psalm 34:19). Righteous people have many afflictions, but notice that God delivers them *"out of them all."* Was David a good man? Yes. However, God made him a better man through the abundance of difficulties that he endured. More troubles should lead to greater faith in God. Your problems at home, in your neighborhood, at work, or in church are designed to draw you closer to Him.

A Protecting Furnace

Though the furnace may be painful, it is still a safe place for the Christian. The prophet reminds us, *"...when thou walkest through the fire, thou shalt not be burned; neither shall the flame kindle upon thee"* (Isaiah 43:2). The flame has limited power, and we can be sure that God's furnaces are meant to refine us, not destroy us. Daniel's three companions, give us ample proof of this. They were righteous men who were thrown into a burning fiery furnace by a heathen king, but they felt no harm. When the king saw that God had miraculously delivered them, he proclaimed, *"Lo, I see four men loose, walking in the midst of the fire, and they have no hurt; and the form of the fourth is like the Son of God"* (Daniel 3:25). The young men were safe because Jesus was with them! What reassurance it is that the Lord will protect us when we face the furnace of affliction. It is better to be in a place of difficulty with God than anywhere else without Him. If you are in a time of testing, realize that the Lord is *"walking in the midst of the fire"* with you. He will deliver you.

> You are not alone in the furnace.

A Purposeful Furnace

For the Christian, affliction is not mere happenstance. The Lord has a specific purpose in mind each time we pass through the furnace. Let's consider two results He may have in mind for your trial.

First, the furnace purifies. God told Israel, *"I have refined thee...in the furnace of affliction."* As fire burns the impurities found in precious metals, so the furnace is designed to remove pollutants in God's children. When we are purged from sinful influences, we become *"meet for the master's use, and prepared unto every good work"*

(2 Timothy 2:21). Let us not begrudge our Lord for making us more valuable and useful.

Second, the furnace promotes. The three young men who survived the fiery furnace in Daniel's day were rewarded in the end. Notice what happened, *"Then the king promoted Shadrach, Meshach, and Abednego, in the province of Babylon"* (Daniel 3:30). The furnace of affliction was used to promote them. The Lord often uses trials to strengthen us for bigger and better things. As the fires of a kiln make bricks harder, so the furnace of affliction makes us stronger. Like the three young men, we will be happy in the end when God uses the furnace to strengthen and promote us. All is well that ends well. Truly, God's trials are purposeful.

A Practical Furnace

When the Lord looks for servants to use in a special way, where does He begin His search? In the entertainment room where saints are distracted by worldly pleasures? In the banqueting room where they are filling their appetites? In the lounge where they are busy relaxing? In the bedroom where they are fast asleep? No to all of the above! He finds His choicest servants in the furnace room. Did He not say, *"I have chosen thee in the furnace of affliction"*?

In 1678, one of the most influential Christian books ever written was published, *The Pilgrim's Progress*. For years, it was second in popularity only to the Bible, having been translated into over two hundred languages. When the Lord wanted such a book written, where did He find its author? It was not in a palace or on a playground. John

Bunyan was in prison suffering for his faith. It was affliction, not affluence or amusement that made Bunyan useful. We often long for a life of comfort and ease, but that is not what prepares us for the Lord's service. The Son of God was made *"perfect through sufferings"* (Hebrews 2:10). Since the servant is not above his Lord, we must expect to suffer as Christ did. As God used Bunyan's troubles for His glory, He wants to do the same with yours. Trust the Lord to use your trials to further His work.

Conclusion

Are you presently in the furnace of affliction? Whether your adversities are to purify you of sin or to sanctify you for greater usefulness, allow God to accomplish His will. He has a purpose for every trial, and you must trust Him. If you endure affliction, you become a prime candidate to be chosen for a special task. The furnace of affliction is the place where the Lord has shaped and formed some of His finest servants. Those who have suffered the most have often been used the most. Are you willing to go through the flames of refinement to bring more glory to the Lord? When commenting on the furnace of affliction, C. H. Spurgeon drew this conclusion, "We choose the furnace, since God chooses us in it."[8] Oh, for that kind of faith!

---

[8] Charles H. Spurgeon, *Faith's Checkbook* (Ross-shire, Scotland: Christian Focus Publications, 2009), 240.

Day Twenty Seven

Give Thanks

"In every thing give thanks: for this is the will of God in Christ Jesus concerning you" —1 Thessalonians 5:18.

Disappointments tend to lead to discontentment. When it begins to rain during your picnic, you will usually hear more grumbling than gratitude. Try telling a young child that he cannot go outside and play until his chores are done. You are more likely to hear a dejected, "Oh, ma!" than a jubilant, "Oh, goodie!" We tend to be more cheerful on bright, sunny days than on dark, cloudy ones. The truth is that we are more prone to pout than praise when difficulties arise. When trouble overwhelms us, the last thing we feel like doing is being thankful. Sometimes we think that we deserve to complain about our circumstances. We even believe that murmuring will make us feel better, but it never does. The solution is quite simple—be thankful.

Giving Thanks Is Simple, But Not Easy

Though the solution to our despondency may be simple, it is also difficult. When tragedy strikes, it is not easy to be filled with gratitude. For instance, losing a loved one can cause deep pain and sorrow. How can we possibly be expected to be thankful when we lose someone that is dear to us? Let us ask another question. How will complaining about our loss make us feel better? It won't. However, when we follow God's plan of being thankful, we focus on the Lord instead of on our loss. Your heart will be blessed by thanking God for the wonderful memories that you have of your loved one and the time you had together. Jesus told the disciples that they would mourn after His death, but He also promised, *"...your sorrow shall be turned into joy"* (John 16:20). God specializes in replacing our sorrow with joy! Heartfelt thankfulness immediately puts our hearts in tune with the Lord.

Giving Thanks Brings Us Close to God

When all is dim, we need the radiance of God's presence to cheer us. Few things usher us into the presence of God quicker than thankfulness. Notice how the psalmist said that we should approach the Lord— *"Enter into his gates with thanksgiving, and into his courts with praise"* (Psalm 100:4). As we give thanks, we gain the attention of the Lord and prepare our hearts to commune with Him. David's prayer reveals why it is important to get close to God in our times of sorrow. He said, *"...in thy presence is fulness of joy"* (Psalm 16:11). When we become thankful, we draw closer to God and experience the comfort that only He can give.

Giving Thanks Is God's Will

You may say, "I don't feel very thankful." Give thanks anyway. Paul reminds us, *"In every thing give thanks: for this is the will of God."* Giving thanks is part of God's will for your life. Disobeying God always has negative consequences, which only make your situation worse. As parents, we often tell our children to do things that they may not want to do because we know that those things are good for them. God is no different. He knows what is best for us, and that is why He instructs us to be thankful. If we refuse to give thanks, we forfeit the peace that God wants to provide. Notice also that we are to be thankful in every situation—*"In every thing give thanks."* Since we need the Lord's help in our trials, it makes sense to thank Him especially when times are tough. Even in your darkest hours, you can find something for which to be thankful. Matthew Henry was a notable preacher and author in his day. One evening, after being robbed, he wrote in his diary, "Let me be thankful first, because I was never robbed before; second, because, although they took my purse, they did not take my life; third, because although they took my all, it was not much; and fourth, because it was I who was robbed, and not I who robbed."[9] This kind of attitude not only pleases God but also enables us to have a brighter outlook on life. Those who fail to be thankful usually develop a bitter spirit, and that leads to more problems.

| Faithlessness produces thanklessness. |

Giving Thanks Is a Spiritual Indicator

Strife and bitterness are characteristics of carnal people, but thankfulness is a trait found in Spirit-filled believers. In Ephesians 5:18-20, God not only commanded us to *"be*

---

[9] Walter B. Knight, *Knight's Master Book of 4,000 Illustrations* (Grand Rapids: William B. Eerdmans Publishing Company, 1956), 682.

filled with the Spirit" but also mentioned that being grateful is an evidence of His filling—*"Giving thanks always for all things unto God and the Father in the name of our Lord Jesus Christ."* When we refuse to give *"thanks always for all things,"* it indicates that we are walking in the flesh instead of walking in the Spirit. The only thing we can expect from living a carnal life is more sin and more misery. Therefore, when we face disappointments in life, let our hearts be filled with thankfulness instead of complaints.

Conclusion

Nobody can avoid times of trouble, but we can choose how we react to them. Though it is easier to complain, it only makes matters worse. Let us resolve to turn to the Lord with grateful hearts and seek His assistance. Paul exhorts, *"Be careful for nothing; but in every thing by prayer and supplication with thanksgiving let your requests be made known unto God"* (Philippians 4:6). Your heavenly Father knows your plight and is eager to help you. So, follow His plan. Worry about nothing, pray about everything, and give thanks in all things. What a wonderful solution for all of our problems!

Day Twenty Eight

The Path to Discouragement

"...the soul of the people was much discouraged because of the way" —Numbers 21:4.

Few of us intentionally start down the path that leads to discouragement. We try to keep a bright outlook on life, but trials sometimes get the best of us. When that happens, we find that discouragement leads to other problems. This was the case with the children of Israel when they were in the wilderness. Let's learn some lessons from them so that we can avoid the same fate that they suffered.

The Cause of Discouragement

The reason Israel fell into despair was because they had taken their eyes off the Lord and focused on their circumstances. Our text reveals, *"...the soul of the people was much discouraged because of the way."* The word *way* refers to the road upon which they were travelling. Simply put, life had become difficult.

Israel had just mourned the death of one of their leaders, Aaron. Then they were attacked by the forces of Arad, a Canaanite king. Though the Lord had given Israel a great victory over Arad, the men of war were tired. They had travelled 80 miles on foot to destroy Arad's cities and 80 miles back to Mt. Hor. From there, they had another 60 miles to go with the entire congregation of Israel before entering the Promised Land. The journey through life may seem long and tiresome, but we must not allow fatigue to discourage us.

Israel had forgotten that they were on the path to the Promised Land! After 40 years of wandering in the wilderness, they were soon to enjoy God's promised blessings. Instead of looking ahead with excitement, they were focused on their present problems. Isn't that how we are at times? We forget that we are marching on the path to victory and start looking at all of our troubles. Discouragement focuses on today's problems instead of tomorrow's blessings. How sad that they were *"discouraged because of the way."* The way, though difficult, led to abundant blessings. Always remember that the end of God's path more than makes up for any hardships suffered along the way. Paul reminds us, *"For I reckon that the sufferings of this present time are not worthy to be compared with the glory which shall be revealed in us"* (Romans 8:18).

| Look past present troubles and envision God's blessings. |

Notice also that discouragement grows. The people had become *"much discouraged."* With each step, the Israelites had become more disheartened. We don't go from victory to great discouragement in one step. It is a gradual process. Once we start focusing on negative things, we become more discontent as time goes on. That is why it is important to stop dwelling on problems and look ahead for God's blessing. If you have found yourself getting down because of the way, snap out of it before it leads to more trouble.

The Consequences of Discouragement

When we get on the highway to hopelessness, the final destination is not discouragement. Sin always takes us farther than we had planned to travel. One sin typically leads to another. People who become discouraged eventually become disgruntled. They are unhappy, irritated, and full of complaints. That is what happened to Israel. Notice the consequences of discouragement found in Numbers 21.

First, we become disgruntled with God's Person. In Israel's mind, the Lord was the source of their problems. After all, they encountered their troubles because they had followed Him. Therefore, they were upset with Him. His will was no longer their will. Instead of turning to the Lord in their trouble, they turned against Him—*"the people spake against God"* (21:5). This happens far too often with Christians. Have you spoken against the Lord or blamed Him for your trouble? Since God is the only One Who can help in our crisis, we should be very careful not to harden our hearts against Him.

Second, we become disgruntled with God's preacher. The children of Israel were upset with Moses—*"the people spake...against Moses"* (21:5). When people are out of sorts with God, they end up having trouble with His spokesmen too. Discouragement can cause us to start blaming others for our problems. Unfortunately, we tend to transfer our frustration with God to our spiritual leaders. Lashing out at those who follow God and care for us will never help us. If you are discouraged, deal with it Biblically before you hurt important relationships in your life.

Third, we become disgruntled with God's plan. The Lord brought Israel out of Egypt because He loved them. He delivered them from bondage and intended to bring them to a land flowing with milk and honey. However, that is not what the Israelites thought. They said, *"ye brought us up out of Egypt to die in the wilderness"* (21:5). Discouragement skewed their thinking so much that they totally misunderstood God's plan for their lives. The Lord wanted them to enjoy a better life, but they thought He had taken it away from them. When you are on God's path, the way may become bumpy, but abundant blessings are waiting at the end of the journey.

Fourth, we become disgruntled with God's power. Because the children of Israel had turned against God, they forgot about His power. The Lord had previously showed His ability to provide for their needs. Despite receiving manna from heaven and water from the rock, they complained about their present lack of food and water. Surely, God was powerful enough to help them again! However, they said, *"there is no bread, neither is there any water"* (21:5). Discouragement robs us of hope and causes us to doubt God's power to work as He did in the past. It causes us to doubt His power to help us today.

Fifth, we become disgruntled with God's provision. The Israelites were not satisfied with what God had provided for them. They ate for 40 years in the wilderness without having to cultivate, plant, or harvest. The manna that the Lord provided was so heavenly that it was called angel's food. However, God's people saw it differently because they were discouraged. Instead of being thankful, they complained, saying, *"our soul loatheth this light bread"* (21:5). In other words, they hated what God had given them! Be careful not to go down the path of discouragement because you will despise the good things God has already bestowed upon you. Because continuing on the path to discouragement destroys our fellowship with the Lord, He will take action to get our attention.

The Correction of Discouragement

When we get so discouraged that we are no longer content with God's will, we ask for trouble. God administered swift, severe discipline to Israel for being ungrateful—*"And the LORD sent fiery serpents among the people, and they bit the people; and much people of Israel died"* (21:6). As a boy, I remember my father saying, "If you want to complain, I will give you something to complain about." Years later, I see that my dad was not the first one to have that philosophy. The Lord works the same way. Israel had enjoyed God's blessings in the wilderness. Now they were on the road to the Promised Land, but all they could do was complain. Therefore, God afflicted them so that they would turn back to Him.

Notice that God's correction was *painful*—*"the LORD sent fiery serpents."* The word *fiery* refers to burning, which appears to describe the unbearable pain that the poisonous venom inflicted upon the people. God's rod of chastisement stings! Be careful not to go too far down the path of discouragement, or you may find it more troubling than you had expected.

Consider also that God's correction can be *permanent*—*"much people of Israel died."* Some died because they failed to repent and seek the Lord. God wanted to heal them, but they first had to turn back to Him. It is sad to see some Christians become so bitter against God that they have no intentions to seek His help. The longer we resist the Lord in our times of trouble, the more we stand to lose.

See also that God's correction was *productive*. It produced a few things in the lives of the children of Israel. First, we see confession—*"the people came to Moses, and said, We have sinned, for we have spoken against the* LORD, *and against thee"* (21:7). God wants us to be specific and name our offenses. Second, we observe intercession—*"Moses prayed for the people"* (21:7). Thankfully, the man of God was willing to forgive those who had gone against him. If you have hurt your relationship with a spiritual leader, humble yourself and apologize.

> God wants to restore you, not destroy you.

You may be surprised to find him more willing to forgive than you realize. Third, we notice restoration—*"And Moses made a serpent of brass, and put it upon a pole, and it came to pass, that if a serpent had bitten any man, when he beheld the serpent of brass, he lived"* (21:9). The Lord wanted them to live, not die. He provided a way of salvation for them. Though our sin may bring pain and heartache to our lives, God is willing to heal us and restore us to fellowship with Him when we repent. Fourth, we see determination—*"And the children of Israel set forward"* (21:10). The people got back on the path toward the Promised Land with no more complaints. As a result, the

Lord brought them to a well, which supplied water for their thirst. Moving forward for God puts us back on the path to His blessings. Finally, we observe jubilation—*"Then Israel sang this song, Spring up, O well; sing ye unto it"* (21:17). The Lord's chastening brought them out of the pit of discouragement and caused them to rejoice in His blessings. Their pouting turned to praising. Oh, that we would allow God's correction to change us too! When we shake off our discouragement, we will see the Lord's provision in a new light.

Conclusion

When we travel on the path that God has chosen for us, we march toward victory. How sad when we focus on our troubles instead of God's promised blessings! If we allow ourselves to become discouraged, other sins will soon follow. We will be upset with God and His men. We will think He is against us instead of being for us. We will fail to trust Him to provide for us and complain about what He has done for us. If you are on the path to discouragement, get off it before the Lord has to correct you.

"For I will be merciful to their unrighteousness, and their sins and their iniquities will I remember no more" —*Hebrews 8:12.*

Day Twenty Nine

Feeling Guilty

"...this one thing I do, forgetting those things which are behind, and reaching forth unto those things which are before, I press toward the mark for the prize of the high calling of God in Christ Jesus" —Philippians 3:13-14.

Everbody has guilty feelings at times. Guilt refers to the state of having committed an offense or crime. Some offenses are more serious than others. For example, there is a huge difference between cheating on one's diet and cheating on one's spouse. A person ought to feel much more guilt over ruining their marriage than over spoiling their weight loss program. Unfortunately, some people are prone to beat themselves up over minor offenses like blowing their diet. They have a difficult time coping with any failure, whether it is large or small, because they set high expectations for themselves. Further, they tend to second-guess themselves and live with regrets over past decisions. Such an outlook on life leads to discouragement and defeat.

Confusion About Guilt

Since we all struggle with guilt in one form or another, let's consider if guilt is good or bad. Guilty feelings can actually be both good and bad. They are good when they cause people to repent of wrongdoing and change their ways. They are bad when they are found in someone who has done nothing wrong. Guilty feelings are also bad when they linger in someone who has been forgiven. The apostle Paul was concerned about a man in the church of Corinth who had repented of his sin but was in danger of being *"swallowed up with overmuch sorrow"* (2 Corinthians 2:7). God does not want His people to be constantly filled with remorse and regret.

Since guilt is associated with a crime or offense, it would be helpful to consider how it works in our relationship with God. When we break God's laws, we are guilty—*"Now we know that what things soever the law saith, it saith to them who are under the law: that every mouth may be stopped, and all the world may become guilty before God"* (Romans 3:19). The Ten Commandments were not given as a means to become righteous. On the contrary, they show us our sinfulness. As we compare our lives to God's Law, we *"become guilty before God."* Once we acknowledge our guilt, we see our need to turn to Jesus for forgiveness. Having a sense of guilt is good when it brings us to repentance.

Responding to Guilt

Unfortunately, not everyone responds to guilt properly. Some people refuse to admit their guilt. Others acknowledge it but have no remorse for their actions. Even worse, some shrug off the conviction of God and harden their hearts against Him. Paul described such people as having *"their conscience seared with a hot iron"* (1 Timothy

4:2). In other words, a person's conscience can become calloused, causing a loss of sensation. Though he is guilty of offending God, he has lost a deep sense of his guilt.

Just like there are guilty people who do not feel guilty, there are people who have sought forgiveness but still feel guilty. They find themselves confessing the same sin several times but still feeling dirty. Their conscience is plagued and their soul is darkened. Life is miserable. Does that describe you at times? The Lord does not want any of His children to battle a never ending sense of guilt.

We must remember that there is a difference between being guilty and feeling guilty. Committing the offense makes us guilty. Confessing our sin brings cleansing. *"If we confess our sins, he is faithful and just to forgive us our sins, and to cleanse us from all unrighteousness"* (1 John 1:9). Once we have, in faith, asked God to forgive us, we are no longer guilty. The offense is washed away, leaving nothing to feel guilty about. Some people fall into the trap of repeatedly confessing the same sin, hoping that their efforts will appease God. That is not faith. We must take God at His Word and believe that He will forgive us the first time we confess our sin. You and I are not supposed to be our own defense attorneys, pleading our cases. That is what Christ does for us—*"And if any man sin, we have an advocate with the Father, Jesus Christ the righteous"* (1 John 2:1). When you have sinned, confess it and trust that Jesus will represent you well. He has never lost a case!

> Guilt is gone once we have, in faith, confessed our sins.

When God forgives, He also forgets. Consider His wonderful promise, *"For I will be merciful to their* unrighteousness, and their sins and their iniquities will I remember no more" (Hebrews 8:12). If God remembers our sins no more, neither should we! In some cases, you may need to make things right with people you have offended; but once you have done your part, you can enjoy a clear conscience.

Victory Over Guilt

Paul learned two important truths that helped him to cope with his past failures. If you struggle with guilt, taking these two steps will help you have victory too.

First, do not dwell on the past. No amount of self-inflicted pain or sorrow will change the past. Torturing yourself with endless scenarios such as "I should have..." or "I should not have..." is not helpful. Sure, we should learn from our mistakes but not dwell on them. If God has chosen to forget your sin, you must choose to do likewise. Satan loves to continually remind us of our shortcomings, but we must not listen to him. It's time to say like Paul, *"...this one thing I do, forgetting those things which are behind."* If you allow yourself to continually dwell on negative things, you will be weakened instead of empowered. You can ruin a perfectly good future by dwelling on the past. Although you may have to live with the consequences of your sin, you do not have to continue to carry the burden of guilt upon your shoulders. Jesus said, *"Come unto me, all ye that labour and are heavy laden, and I will give you rest."* (Matthew 11:28) Why not enjoy the rest that the Savior promises?

Second, move on with life. Not only did Paul forget his past failures, he learned to focus on productive activities, saying, *"I press toward the mark for the prize of the high calling of God in Christ Jesus."* God wants us to look forward, not backward. Those running in a race focus on the finish line, not what is behind them. When runners turn around, they lose their stride and get off course. Unfortunately, Christians do the same thing by focusing on past failures. The devil loves to distract us with our past to prevent us from pressing toward the mark. Rather than focusing on what you were, concentrate on what God wants you to become. Believe it or not, you have great potential to be used of the Lord despite past failures. Though Paul had committed hideous sins in his past, God used him in great ways. He penned much of the New Testament, won many souls to Christ, and provided an example of holiness to follow. If God used him after committing horrible sins, He can use you too. Shake off any discouragement you have concerning former days and determine to do your best from this point on. It is time to let go of guilt that has already been forgiven.

Conclusion

When a Christian is forgiven, he is no longer guilty in the eyes of God. If you still struggle with guilt after being forgiven, you either still have sin that needs to be confessed, or you doubt God's promise to forgive and forget. If you have not dealt with your sin Biblically, you should feel guilty. However, if you have repented of it, you are no longer guilty. Any feelings of guilt you have after being forgiven are based on imaginary guilt.

Have you allowed guilt to needlessly linger in your heart? If you have done wrong, confess it to God and make things right with your fellow man. Then, move on. Refuse to live in the past. Stop condemning yourself for all of your failures. When God forgives, He forgets. Refuse to dwell on what God has forgotten!

Day Thirty

Why Are You Troubled?

"Why art thou cast down, O my soul? and why art thou disquieted within me? hope thou in God: for I shall yet praise him, who is the health of my countenance, and my God" —Psalm 42:11.

The psalmist records a conversation that he had with himself. His heart was broken, and he found no comfort in his tears. Crying may offer a temporary release of emotion, but it has no healing power of its own. His soul was no better for its grief, and neither will yours be.

Being *cast down* refers to sinking in despair. To have a disquieted soul implies inner noise and commotion. Does that describe you? Are you depressed in spirit and lacking peace within your heart? If so, ask yourself the same question that the psalmist asked himself, *"Why?"* Perhaps your answer might be that you have suffered great loss, mistreatment, failure, or pain. Whatever the cause, it matters not. Being cast down will not fix the problem but only make it worse. Your pain and grief may be real. It was real to the writer of this psalm, but instead of continuing in his sorrow, he found a solution. Let's briefly consider a few thoughts from this psalm.

Heartache

Notice that the writer experienced heartache. He longed for relief of his trouble and a visitation from God. He felt as though the Lord had hidden His face in his affliction. He cried, *"My soul thirsteth for God, for the living God: when shall I come and appear before God?"* (Psalm 42:2). Does it seem that your prayers for comfort and respite go unanswered at times? This is not the time to stop praying! All the more we must rightly set our attention and affections upon the One Who alone can deliver us.

Hurt

The psalmist suffered hurt. He experienced tears and taunting. Listen to the anguish in his heart—*"My tears have been my meat day and night, while they continually say unto me, Where is thy God?"* (Psalm 42:3). It may be that someone has hurt you in like manner, or perhaps the pain comes because someone is unable to understand your heartache. When such grief is *"day and night,"* it is time to discover the reason hope has not been restored. The psalmist was able to identify why he had not gotten over his sorrow. It may be the same reason you continue to struggle. Instead of casting his burden upon the Lord, he was carrying it himself. He admitted, *"When I remember these things, I pour out my soul in me"* (Psalm 42:4). If we are to pour out our soul, it must be to God, not to self. The more we rehearse our troubles to ourselves, the more miserable we will become.

> Looking within brings heartache, not hope.

Help

What the psalmist needed was help. He finally realized that if he was going to talk to himself, he ought to be constructive. Instead of tormenting his heart, he decided to ask some worthwhile questions. He began by asking what good it was doing him to be depressed—*"Why art thou cast down, O my soul? and why art thou disquieted in me?"* (Psalm 42:5). His self-interrogation yielded immediate results. His next statement provided the solution, *"hope thou in God."*

Hope

Each of us needs hope. The psalmist concluded that he would look to God instead of looking within. He prayed, *"O my God, my soul is cast down within me: therefore will I remember thee"* (Psalm 42:6). How much better it is to remember the Savior than our sadness! Another psalm records another source for our hope, *"I wait for the LORD, my soul doth wait, and in his word do I hope"* (Psalm 130:5). By meditating on the precious promises of the Almighty, we will be renewed in the inner man. The apostle Paul adds that we *"may abound in hope, through the power of the Holy Ghost"* (Romans 15:13). We must confess our sin of self-pity and seek a fresh filling of God's Spirit. He is called the Comforter, and He will certainly live up to His name! Oh yes, hope is available. Lift your eyes upward and hope will be renewed. Each time you begin to falter, repeat the steps listed above. They have worked countless times for a multitude of saints, and they will work for you.

Before ending our discussion of hope, let us see what we can expect from God when we truly seek Him. *"Yet the LORD will command his lovingkindness in the daytime, and in the night his song shall be with me"* (Psalm 42:8). A blessing was promised for each moment. In the business of the day, we can expect kindness. In the darkness of night, God puts a song in the heart of all who trust Him. The psalmist then promised, *"...prayer unto the God of my life"* (Psalm 42:8). Be sure to praise God for the goodness He extends to your soul. When He makes you happy, bring Him joy with a prayer of thanksgiving.

Once hope is restored, we regain our spiritual *health*. Though the battle continued to rage for the psalmist, he was now able to pray with confidence. In the face of trouble, he now had expectation instead of despair. He exclaimed, *"I shall yet praise him, who is the health of my countenance, and my God"* (Psalm 42:11). A hopeful heart is a healthy heart, and a healthy heart is a hopeful heart. The psalmist had found the remedy for his soul. God changed his countenance, and He can change yours, too!

There is no good reason to be down in the dumps when God is still on the throne. Hope in God. Focus on Providence instead of your problems. May the Lord heal your hurt and heartache, replacing it with continual hope!

The Serenity Prayer

God grant me the serenity
To accept the things I cannot change;
Courage to change the things I can;
And wisdom to know the difference.
—Reinhold Neibuhr, 1892-1971

Day Thirty One

Renewed

"For which cause we faint not; but though our outward man perish, yet the inward man is renewed day by day"
—2 Corinthians 4:16.

Our journey together is almost over. We have studied God's solutions to many of life's problems. Without a doubt, the Bible renews faith and restores hope. Hopefully, the truths we have discussed have helped you to focus on the Lord instead of your troubles. You must remember, however, that problems are a part of life. If you have struggled with grief, discouragement, fear, anxiety, bitterness, or other wrong attitudes, they will likely return in the future. Rather than worrying about their recurrence, it is better to prepare for them. That is done by continually renewing the *"inward man."*

The word *renew* means "to make new, renovate, or restore." When we receive Christ as Savior, the Lord saves us *"by the washing of regeneration, and renewing of the Holy Ghost"* (Titus 3:5). He changes us within and gives us a new nature. However, because we still have a corrupt flesh, we are tempted to yield to its negative influences. The problems that life throws at us can distract us. Once we get our eyes off the Lord, we begin to be overwhelmed by our troubles. We worry, withdraw, and wonder how things will work out. When the apostle Paul described the battle that he had with his flesh, he cried out, *"O wretched man that I am!"* (Romans 7:24). Thankfully, we have hope. To combat our natural weaknesses, we need supernatural help. Therefore, we are instructed that *"the inward man"* must be *"renewed day by day."* Praise God that our faith and hope can be restored on a daily basis! Let's consider some particulars about renewing the inner man.

The Place of Renewal

Where do negative thoughts reside? They dwell in the mind. The mind is the battlefield where the devil likes to attack us most. Therefore, that is the area we must guard. Peter said, *"Wherefore gird up the loins of your mind"* (1 Peter 1:13). In Peter's day, people understood what it meant to gird something. Soldiers wore belts to gather up their robes above their knees, making it easier to maneuver in battle. To gird up the loins of the mind means to get ready to fight. It involves gathering up our loose thoughts and allowing nothing to trip up our thinking. Don't fall for Satan's stumbling blocks of fear, worry, and bitterness. Control your mind and refuse to dwell on negative thoughts.

> The mind is a battlefield. Guard it.

Paul instructed, *"And be renewed in the spirit of your mind"* (Ephesians 4:23). Since the mind controls our actions, it is important that we think correctly. Let's consider an example. When a woman loses her husband, she struggles with grief. It is natural for her to grieve because of her loss, but if she dwells on her suffering instead of focusing on the Lord, she will develop wrong thought patterns. Soon, wrong actions will follow. She is likely to become discouraged, self-centered, and bitter. She may even withdraw from family and friends and wallow in self-pity. When that happens, even people who try to cheer her up will not enjoy her company. How miserable we can become when we fail to renew our minds! Hopefully, you see how important it is to prevent wrong thoughts to linger in your mind.

The way to change our lives is to renew our minds. Once again, Paul gave some helpful advice. He said, *"...be ye transformed by the renewing of your mind."* (Romans 12:2). A transformed life comes from renewed thinking. Next, we will see how to renew our minds.

The Process of Renewal

The Lord gives us three tools to use to renew our minds: His Word, prayer, and faithfulness. Each one is important and cannot be neglected. To illustrate this, let's consider a simple recipe. If you want to make buttermilk biscuits, you need three ingredients: self-rising flour, shortening, and buttermilk. If you neglect to add one of the ingredients, you will fail to have biscuits. In the same manner, if you want to be renewed, you must follow God's recipe. Let's consider each ingredient that God gives for renewal.

First, begin with the Bible. Notice that *"the new man...is renewed in knowledge after the image of him that created him"* (Colossians 3:10). How do we get knowledge of our Creator? We get it by reading the Bible. As we study God's Word, we discover that He is longsuffering, kind, loving, holy, merciful, forgiving, just, temperate, and so much more! Consider what Paul said about seeing God's glory through the pages of Scripture—*"But we all, with open face beholding as in a glass the glory of the Lord, are changed into the same image from glory to glory, even as by the Spirit of the Lord"* (2 Corinthians 3:18). The Bible changes us into God's image! The Spirit of God uses the Word of God to make us more like the Son of God. If we saturate our minds with God's Word, we will become more like Christ. That enables us to maintain proper attitudes when facing hardships and heartaches.

Second, mix in prayer. The Bible is only one element of renewal. When David had lost his peace and joy, he prayed in desperation to be restored to close fellowship with the Lord. He cried out, *"Create in me a clean heart, O God; and renew a right spirit within me"* (Psalm 51:10). The words *"O God"* indicate his earnest desire. Prayer ought to be more than a routine; it must be heartfelt. When we pray with dependence upon the Lord, we can expect Him to intervene. David did not pray sporadically. He committed himself to seek the Lord throughout each day. He said, *"Evening, and morning, and at noon, will I pray, and cry aloud: and he shall hear my voice"* (Psalm 55:17). Because he prayed much, he expected much. He was assured that God would hear him—*"he shall hear my voice."* A vibrant prayer life will keep your heart right and renewed. Once you begin to be a faithful prayer warrior, when doubts and fears assail, you will naturally take your troubles directly to the throne of

> When troubles rise, so should our prayers.

grace to *"find grace to help in time of need"* (Hebrews 4:16).

Third, add faithfulness. Reading the Bible and praying are good, but they must be done consistently. Occasional fellowship with God does not produce long-term results. Since we sin daily, we need to be renewed daily. God clearly states that *"the inward man is renewed day by day."* Just as we eat daily to maintain our strength, we are to partake of God's Word every day. Yesterday's communion with God was good for yesterday, but we need help today too. It must be *"day by day."* Be faithful to spend time with God each day, but don't limit it to a single devotional time. Success is granted to the ones who *"meditate"* in the Bible *"day and night"* (Joshua 1:8). It is said of the blessed man, *"...his delight is in the law of the* LORD; *and in his law doth he meditate day and night"* (Psalm 1:2). The way to be happy and look past your troubles is to repeatedly meditate on God's Word all through the day. Along with faithful Bible reading, learn to maintain an attitude of prayer throughout every day. That's what it means to *"Pray without ceasing"* (1 Thessalonians 5:17). Whisper a prayer any time you sense a need for divine help or fellowship! When we put all of the ingredients together (the Bible, prayer, and faithfulness), we will be prepared when negative thinking starts to creep back into our lives.

The Products of Renewal

If we faithfully renew our minds through prayer and meditation upon God's Word, we can change how we handle life's disappointments. Consider what a renewed mind produces.

First, a renewed mind cultivates right thoughts. The believers in Philippi were warned, *"Be careful for nothing"* (Philippians 4:6). As we have seen previously, the word *careful* refers to being anxious. Instead of worrying, Paul told the people to engage in *"prayer…with thanksgiving"* (Philippians 4:6). What would be the result? They would have *"the peace of God"* protecting their *"hearts and minds"* (Philippians 4:7). In other words, after renewing their minds, they would be able to think positively. Notice what they were able to focus on after their minds were restored—*"…whatsoever things are true, whatsoever things are honest, whatsoever things are just, whatsoever things are pure, whatsoever things are lovely, whatsoever things are of good report; if there be any virtue, and if there be any praise, think on these things"* (Philippians 4:8). Once we focus on the Lord, He protects our *"hearts and minds"* and enables us to think positively instead of negatively. Even if you are prone to wrong thoughts, God can change them!

| A renewed mind is a protected mind. |

Second, a renewed mind yields right actions. King Solomon made a wise observation about man, *"For as he thinketh in his heart, so is he"* (Proverbs 23:7). As we know, thoughts lead to actions. Ralph Waldo Emmerson expanded upon that truth, saying, "Sow a thought and you reap an action; sow an act and you reap a habit; sow a habit and you reap a character; sow a character and you reap a destiny." In other words, by changing our thoughts, we can change our future. If you are prone to living a defeated and discouraged life, there's hope! God loves to change our dispositions.

In Queen Esther's day, the Jewish people were doomed and faced annihilation. After they fasted and prayed, God intervened and spared their lives. In the end, the Lord made them victorious over their enemies. Truly, God turned *"sorrow to joy"* and *"mourning into a good day"* (Esther 9:22). Once their thinking changed, their actions did too. Instead of living in fear, they were happy and able to rejoice—they had *"days of feasting and joy, and of sending portions one to another, and gifts to the poor"* (Esther 9:22). What the Lord did for them, He can do for you! With a renewed mind, you will begin to praise God and be a blessing to others as they did in Esther's day. That's a lot better than focusing on your miseries!

> God can turn sorrow into joy.

Third, a renewed mind produces a right attitude. When our spirit suffers, it is difficult to maintain hope. Solomon said, *"The spirit of a man will sustain his infirmity; but a wounded spirit who can bear?"* (Proverbs 18:14). A wounded spirit is one that is afflicted and broken. David found himself in such a condition. We would do well to seek a remedy as he did. He prayed, *"...renew a right spirit within me"* (Psalm 51:10). Though his soul had been brought low, he knew the Lord could restore it. God loves to lift our spirits—*"He raiseth up the poor out of the dust"* (Psalm 113:7). If you are poor in spirit, Jesus can make you happy. He said, *"Blessed are the poor in spirit"* (Matthew 5:3). Fear, discouragement, and bitterness cannot coexist with a *"right spirit."* You can be delivered from a melancholy mood. So, renew your mind and begin to enjoy a changed attitude. Oh, how wonderful to be happy again!

Fourth, a renewed mind provides a right outlook. Those who are *"without Christ"* have *"no hope"* (Ephesians 2:12). Therefore, lost people struggle to cope with their problems. They often become angry at God, fail to trust the Lord, rely on drugs and alcohol for relief, and take their frustrations out on others. Unfortunately, some Christians handle their trials the same way. However, we are warned, *"...be not conformed to this world"* (Romans 12:2). We do not have to utterly fail when facing troubles. Instead, we are exhorted, *"...but be ye transformed by the renewing of your mind, that ye may prove what is that good, and acceptable, and perfect, will of God"* (Romans 12:2). Notice that when our minds are renewed, we see things differently. No longer are we at odds with God. We recognize our problems as the *"will of God."* However, even more miraculously, God's will becomes *"good, and acceptable, and perfect"* to us. When you see other believers rejoicing in their time of suffering, it is not because they are super Christians. The reason they have such hope is because they have renewed their minds. Thankfully, you can do the same thing with the same results! A renewed mind allows us to see God's will more clearly. If you are ready to have a brighter outlook, take steps to renew your mind.

> Renewed minds see God's will more clearly.

Conclusion

Problems are part of life. Rather than allow them to defeat you, you can renew your mind. If you have received help from this book, it has been due to the Scriptures contained therein. While it may be helpful to reread parts of this book at times, it is no substitute for digging into the Bible on your own. When doubts, fears, and heartaches return, God's Word will give you the power to focus on the goodness of the Lord instead. Remember that *"the inward man is renewed day by day."* Therefore, by maintaining a daily time of Scripture reading and prayer, you will be transformed and see your hardships as the *"good, and acceptable, and perfect, will of God."* Like David, you will be able to say, *"In the day when I cried thou answeredst me, and strengthenedst me with strength in my soul"* (Psalm 138:3). May the Lord enable you to look beyond today's trials and see brighter days ahead!

"But the path of the just is as the shining light, that shineth more and more unto the perfect day"
-Proverbs 4:18.

"For whosoever shall call upon the name of the Lord shall be saved" -Romans 10:13.

APPENDIX A

Help Begins with Salvation

True help begins with salvation. You may ask, "What is salvation?" The term *saved* means "to be rescued." God wants to rescue you from sin and pending judgment. Notice a few important truths about salvation:

1. **God loves you and wants to help.** At times, you may think that nobody loves you. However, God does. *"For God so loved the world, that he gave his only begotten Son, that whosoever believeth in him should not perish, but have everlasting life"* (John 3:16). Not only does God love you, He wants to bring you into His family.

2. **You need help because of your sin.** Whether you battle anger, bitterness, selfishness, pride, jealousy, a complaining spirit, gossip, or a lack of faith, your real problem is a sin problem. *"For all have sinned, and come short of the glory of God"* (Romans 3:23). Sin is at the heart of every uncontrolled passion that lies within the heart. Jesus said, *"For out of the heart proceed evil thoughts, murders, adulteries, fornications, thefts, false witness, blasphemies..."* (Matthew 15:19). If we want forgiveness, we must first admit that we have

sinned against God. We cannot make excuses or blame others for our actions.

3. **You need help because sin will be judged.** Have you ever felt far from God? The reason is because of your sin. *"But your iniquities have separated between you and your God, and your sins have hid his face from you, that he will not hear"* (Isaiah 59:2). If you die with your sin, that separation will become everlasting. Sinners who fail to repent will be punished in eternal flames. *"And whosoever was not found written in the book of life was cast into the lake of fire"* (Revelation 20:15). Because God loves you, He has made a way for you to escape this horrible punishment.

4. **You cannot help yourself.** Sadly, many people try to fix their own problems without God's help. How often have you said, "I'm not going to do that bad thing again," only to fail? You cannot look within for strength to conquer sin; you need to look up!

5. **Jesus is willing to help.** In order to be saved, you need a Savior. That is where Jesus enters the picture. He knew that man could not save himself. Therefore, He left heaven in order to do what we could not do for ourselves—He paid for our sin. Because all sin has to be punished, Jesus willingly took your punishment upon Himself when He died on the cross. *"For Christ also hath once suffered for sins, the just for the unjust, that he might bring us to God"* (1 Peter 3:18). He wants to forgive you, but you must ask Him to do so.

6. **You must repent and trust Jesus.** Jesus mentioned two requirements to be saved—*"…repent ye, and believe the gospel"* (Mark 1:15). First, we must

"repent," meaning that we change our mind. When we realize that our sin offends God, we should hate it and desire to be cleansed. Second, we must *"believe the gospel."* The gospel refers to Christ's death, burial, and resurrection. If you believe that Jesus died for you and rose again, you can have eternal life.

7. **If you ask Jesus to save you, He will.** Salvation is a gift—*"…the gift of God is eternal life through Jesus Christ our Lord"* (Romans 6:23). Like any gift, you have to receive it; but this gift can only be obtained from Jesus. Because He paid for our sins, it means that we cannot pay for them ourselves. No amount of good works we do can earn forgiveness. Are you ready to accept God's gift of salvation by receiving Jesus as your personal Savior? If so, He is ready to forgive and change you. We are promised, *"For whosoever shall call upon the name of the Lord shall be saved"* (Romans 10:13). You can call upon Him to save you by praying something like this: *Dear Jesus, I know that I have sinned against You and face eternal punishment. I realize that I am powerless to save myself, but I believe You died in my place. Please come into my life and forgive me of all my sin. I trust You alone to change me and save me. Thank You, Jesus. Amen.*

"Whereby are given unto us exceeding great and precious promises: that by these ye might be partakers of the divine nature"

-2 Peter 1:4.

Appendix B

Helpful Verses

The Bible has the answers to all of life's problems. The following verses are arranged under subject headings. Certainly, this is not a comprehensive list, but it can be helpful for those who need help battling harmful emotions.

Anger

He that is soon angry dealeth foolishly: and a man of wicked devices is hated (Proverbs 14:17).

He that is slow to wrath is of great understanding: but he that is hasty of spirit exalteth folly (Proverbs 14:29).

Wherefore, my beloved brethren, let every man be swift to hear, slow to speak, slow to wrath: For the wrath of man worketh not the righteousness of God (James 1:19-20).

Bitterness

Let all bitterness, and wrath, and anger, and clamour, and evil speaking, be put away from you, with all malice: And be ye kind one to another, tenderhearted, forgiving one another, even as God for Christ's sake hath forgiven you (Ephesians 4:31-32).

Looking diligently lest any man fail of the grace of God; lest any root of bitterness springing up trouble you, and thereby many be defiled (Hebrews 12:15).

But if ye have bitter envying and strife in your hearts, glory not, and lie not against the truth (James 3:14).

Fear

And the LORD, he it is that doth go before thee; he will be with thee, he will not fail thee, neither forsake thee: fear not, neither be dismayed (Deuteronomy 31:8).

Yea, though I walk through the valley of the shadow of death, I will fear no evil: for thou art with me; thy rod and thy staff they comfort me (Psalm 23:4).

The LORD is my light and my salvation; whom shall I fear? the LORD is the strength of my life; of whom shall I be afraid? (Psalm 27:1).

Though an host should encamp against me, my heart shall not fear: though war should rise against me, in this will I be confident (Psalm 27:3).

What time I am afraid, I will trust in thee (Psalm 56:3).

The LORD is on my side; I will not fear: what can man do unto me? (Psalm 118:6).

Be not afraid of sudden fear, neither of the desolation of the wicked, when it cometh (Proverbs 3:25).

The fear of man bringeth a snare: but whoso putteth his trust in the LORD shall be safe (Proverbs 29:25).

For God hath not given us the spirit of fear; but of power, and of love, and of a sound mind (2 Timothy 1:7).

So that we may boldly say, The Lord is my helper, and I will not fear what man shall do unto me (Hebrews 13:6).

There is no fear in love; but perfect love casteth out fear: because fear hath torment. He that feareth is not made perfect in love (1 John 4:18).

Hatred

He that saith he is in the light, and hateth his brother, is in darkness even until now... But he that hateth his brother is in darkness, and walketh in darkness, and knoweth not whither he goeth, because that darkness hath blinded his eyes (1 John 2:9, 11).

Hatred stirreth up strifes: but love covereth all sins (Proverbs 10:12).

Better is a dinner of herbs where love is, than a stalled ox and hatred therewith (Proverbs 15:17).

For we ourselves also were sometimes foolish, disobedient, deceived, serving divers lusts and pleasures, living in malice and envy, hateful, and hating one another (Titus 3:3).

Evil shall slay the wicked: and they that hate the righteous shall be desolate (Psalm 34:21).

Hope

Be of good courage, and he shall strengthen your heart, all ye that hope in the LORD (Psalm 31:24).

Behold, the eye of the LORD *is upon them that fear him, upon them that hope in his mercy* (Psalm 33:18).

Let thy mercy, O LORD, *be upon us, according as we hope in thee* (Psalm 33:22).

For in thee, O LORD, *do I hope: thou wilt hear, O Lord my God* (Psalm 38:15).

Why art thou cast down, O my soul? and why art thou disquieted in me? hope thou in God: for I shall yet praise him for the help of his countenance (Psalm 42:5).

But I will hope continually, and will yet praise thee more and more (Psalm 71;14).

My soul fainteth for thy salvation: but I hope in thy word (Psalm 119:81).

Thou art my hiding place and my shield: I hope in thy word (Psalm 119:114).

I wait for the LORD, *my soul doth wait, and in his word do I hope* (Psalm 130:5).

Happy is he that hath the God of Jacob for his help, whose hope is in the LORD *his God* (Psalm 146:5).

The LORD *taketh pleasure in them that fear him, in those that hope in his mercy* (Psalm 147:11).

Rejoicing in hope; patient in tribulation; continuing instant in prayer (Romans 12:12).

For whatsoever things were written aforetime were written for our learning, that we through patience and comfort of the scriptures might have hope (Romans 15:4).

Now the God of hope fill you with all joy and peace in believing, that ye may abound in hope, through the power of the Holy Ghost (Romans 15:13).

To whom God would make known what is the riches of the glory of this mystery among the Gentiles; which is Christ in you, the hope of glory (Colossians 1:27).

But I would not have you to be ignorant, brethren, concerning them which are asleep, that ye sorrow not, even as others which have no hope (1 Thessalonians 4:13).

Looking for that blessed hope, and the glorious appearing of the great God and our Saviour Jesus Christ (Titus 2:13).

Which hope we have as an anchor of the soul, both sure and stedfast, and which entereth into that within the veil (Hebrews 6:19).

Jealousy

And when his brethren saw that their father loved him more than all his brethren, they hated him, and could not speak peaceably unto him (Genesis 37:4).

For jealousy is the rage of a man: therefore he will not spare in the day of vengeance (Proverbs 6:34).

Wrath is cruel, and anger is outrageous; but who is able to stand before envy? (Proverbs 27:4).

Set me as a seal upon thine heart, as a seal upon thine arm: for love is strong as death; jealousy is cruel as the grave: the coals thereof are coals of fire, which hath a most vehement flame (Song of Solomon 8:6).

Peace

I will both lay me down in peace, and sleep: for thou, LORD, only makest me dwell in safety (Psalm 4:8).

The LORD will give strength unto his people; the LORD will bless his people with peace (Psalm 29:11).

Mark the perfect man, and behold the upright: for the end of that man is peace (Psalm 37:37).

Great peace have they which love thy law: and nothing shall offend them (Psalm 119:165).

When a man's ways please the LORD, he maketh even his enemies to be at peace with him (Proverbs 16:7).

For I know the thoughts that I think toward you, saith the LORD, thoughts of peace, and not of evil, to give you an expected end (Jeremiah 29:11).

Peace I leave with you, my peace I give unto you: not as the world giveth, give I unto you. Let not your heart be troubled, neither let it be afraid (John 14:27).

These things I have spoken unto you, that in me ye might have peace. In the world ye shall have tribulation: but be of good cheer; I have overcome the world (John 16:33).

For to be carnally minded is death; but to be spiritually minded is life and peace (Romans 8:6).

Now the God of peace be with you all. Amen (Romans 15:33).

And the God of peace shall bruise Satan under your feet shortly. The grace of our Lord Jesus Christ be with you. Amen (Romans 16:20).

Grace be to you and peace from God the Father, and from our Lord Jesus Christ (Galatians 1:3).

Be careful for nothing; but in every thing by prayer and supplication with thanksgiving let your requests be made known unto God. And the peace of God, which passeth all understanding, shall keep your hearts and minds through Christ Jesus (Philippians 4:6-7).

Pride

Wherefore let him that thinketh he standeth take heed lest he fall (1 Corinthians 10:12).

These six things doth the LORD hate: yea, seven are an abomination unto him: A proud look (Proverbs 6:16-17).

For who maketh thee to differ from another? and what hast thou that thou didst not receive? now if thou didst receive it, why dost thou glory, as if thou hadst not received it? (1 Corinthians 4:7).

When pride cometh, then cometh shame: but with the lowly is wisdom (Proverbs 11:2).

Only by pride cometh contention: but with the well advised is wisdom (Proverbs 13:10).

The LORD will destroy the house of the proud: but he will establish the border of the widow (Proverbs 15:25).

Every one that is proud in heart is an abomination to the LORD: though hand join in hand, he shall not be unpunished (Proverbs 16:5).

Pride goeth before destruction, and an haughty spirit before a fall (Proverbs 16:18).

A man's pride shall bring him low: but honour shall uphold the humble in spirit (Proverbs 29:23).

But he giveth more grace. Wherefore he saith, God resisteth the proud, but giveth grace unto the humble (James 4:6).

Likewise, ye younger, submit yourselves unto the elder. Yea, all of you be subject one to another, and be clothed with humility: for God resisteth the proud, and giveth grace to the humble. Humble yourselves therefore under the mighty hand of God, that he may exalt you in due time (1 Peter 5:5-6).

For all that is in the world, the lust of the flesh, and the lust of the eyes, and the pride of life, is not of the Father, but is of the world (1 John 2:16).

Suicidal Thoughts

Know ye not that ye are the temple of God, and that the Spirit of God dwelleth in you? (1 Corinthians 3:16).

Thou shalt not kill (Exodus 20:13).

And he said unto me, My grace is sufficient for thee: for my strength is made perfect in weakness. Most gladly therefore will I rather glory in my infirmities, that the power of Christ may rest upon me (2 Corinthians 12:9)

I can do all things through Christ which strengtheneth me (Philippians 4:13).

Peace I leave with you, my peace I give unto you: not as the world giveth, give I unto you. Let not your heart be troubled, neither let it be afraid (John 14:27).

These things have I spoken unto you, that my joy might remain in you, and that your joy might be full (John 15:11).

These things I have spoken unto you, that in me ye might have peace. In the world ye shall have tribulation: but be of good cheer; I have overcome the world (John 16:33).

Be not over much wicked, neither be thou foolish: why shouldest thou die before thy time? (Ecclesiastes 7:17).

For thou art my lamp, O LORD: and the LORD will lighten my darkness (2 Samuel 22:29).

Blessed is he whose transgression is forgiven, whose sin is covered (Psalm 32:1).

The righteous cry, and the LORD heareth, and delivereth them out of all their troubles. The LORD is nigh unto them that are of a broken heart; and saveth such as be of a contrite spirit (Psalm 34:17-18).

Be pleased, O LORD, to deliver me: O LORD, make haste to help me (Psalm 40:13).

Why art thou cast down, O my soul? and why art thou disquieted in me? hope thou in God: for I shall yet praise him for the help of his countenance (Psalm 42:5).

Cast thy burden upon the LORD, and he shall sustain thee: he shall never suffer the righteous to be moved (Psalm 55:22).

Thou shalt increase my greatness, and comfort me on every side (Psalm 71:21).

The LORD upholdeth all that fall, and raiseth up all those that be bowed down (Psalm 145:14).

He healeth the broken in heart, and bindeth up their wounds (Psalm 147:3).

Fear thou not; for I am with thee: be not dismayed; for I am thy God: I will strengthen thee; yea, I will help thee; yea, I will uphold thee with the right hand of my righteousness (Isaiah 41:10).

For I the LORD thy God will hold thy right hand, saying unto thee, Fear not; I will help thee (Isaiah 41:13).

Ah Lord GOD! behold, thou hast made the heaven and the earth by thy great power and stretched out arm, and there is nothing too hard for thee (Jeremiah 32:17).

For with God nothing shall be impossible (Luke 1:37).

Casting all your care upon him; for he careth for you (1 Peter 5:7).

...for this day is holy unto our Lord: neither be ye sorry; for the joy of the LORD is your strength (Nehemiah 8:10).

About the Author

Dave Olson became a Baptist preacher in 1993 and has served the Lord in many capacities since that time. After teaching in Bible college, heading up a Christian school, and serving as a pastor, God called Dave into missions. He and his family faithfully served the Lord as missionaries to Zambia, Africa for ten years until a series of ongoing health problems and life-threatening illnesses led to their return in 2012.

In early 2013, the Lord led Dave to focus on a writing ministry, and his books are now used at home and abroad. Dave's experience as an educator and preacher has uniquely equipped him to communicate God's truths to people from every walk of life. In addition to his writing ministry, Dave preaches in revivals, missions conferences, and special meetings across the country.

Visit www.help4Upublications.com for more titles.

Other Titles Available on www.help4Upublications.com

Reading the Word of God is the best way to start your day, and *Daily Light* can make it easier! This book can be used for either personal or family devotions to provide practical insight for daily living. It embarks on a journey through the New Testament, including one thought from an assigned daily Scripture reading designed to share either a challenge or a promise for the day. (204 pages)

Get ready to take a journey through many of the Old Testament books. Morning Light starts in Genesis and includes the books of the Law, History, and Prophets. A practical thought from an assigned daily Scripture reading will challenge you each day. Whether you choose to use Morning Light for personal or family devotions, you will develop a better understanding of the Bible and find practical insight for daily living. (206 pages)

The perfect way to plan your daily devotions! This spiral-bound book contains many devotional helps: prayer list pages, Bible reading schedule, journal pages, topical verse reference, dictionary of archaic words, and more. Great for all ages! (152 pages)

Have you ever wondered what God has to say about finances? It's time to learn the proven principles of Scripture concerning money management. Money by the Book provides Biblical solutions for you and your money. Chapters on contentment, giving, saving, getting out of debt, setting up a budget, teaching your children about money, how to reduce spending, and much more! *Money by the Book* is being used as a textbook in Bible colleges. (246 pages)

www.ingramcontent.com/pod-product-compliance
Lightning Source LLC
Chambersburg PA
CBHW070640050426
42451CB00008B/232